HERTFORDSHIRE C

Hertfordshire Chain Walk

15 Linked walks through rural East Hertfordshire

Published for

East Herts Footpath Society

by

CASTLEMEAD PUBLICATIONS

WARE

First Published in 1987

CASTLEMEAD PUBLICATIONS
Swains Mill, 4A Crane Mead,
Ware, Herts, SG12 9PY

Publishing division of
WARD'S PUBLISHING SERVICES

ISBN 0 948555 12 2

British Library Cataloguing in Publication Data

Hertfordshire Chain Walk : 15 linked walks
through rural east Hertfordshire.
1. East Hertfordshire (Hertfordshire) —
Description and travel — Guide-books
I. East Herts Footpath Society
914.25′8304858 DA670.E1/

ISBN 0-948555-12-2

Set in 10/11 Ehrhardt Roman
by Input Typesetting Ltd, London SW19 8DR
Printed and bound in Great Britain
by Anchor Brendon Limited, Tiptree, Essex

FOREWORD

Footpaths have been important since earliest times, their rights of way jealously guarded by the ordinary people. They existed to link the remoter hamlets – the Ends and Greens – of parishes with churches, their inns, and shops and with the nearest markets. Hence paths overspilled into neighbouring parishes and, as this book demonstrates, it is possible to walk by footpath from the south to the north of Hertfordshire.

In this century when most of us have forsaken the exercise of walking for the speed and comfort of the motor car, the ancient ways are used mainly by enthusiastic ramblers. Bodies like the East Herts Footpath Society, who have cleared many cluttered paths and make representations on the public's behalf to keep paths open, are to be commended.

To all lovers of our beautiful Hertfordshire and of the healthy activity of walking, I have pleasure in recommending this book.

Jack Edwards
(Local Historian)
February 1987

INTRODUCTION

The walks described in this book have been devised as a chain of linking circular walks which stretch from near Crews Hill (BR) Station in the London Borough of Enfield to Ashwell (BR) Station in Cambridgeshire. Each walk is complete in itself and finishes at its starting point. In order to combine two or more walks, linking points have been shown in the maps which appear at the head of each walk description, so that the really ambitious can walk from London to Cambridgeshire (and back!) in this way.

The Society is indebted to a large number of people who have given freely of their time and services to make this book possible. Following conception of the series of walks, volunteers spent a great deal of time planning the routes, which were then walked and re-walked as necessary. The walk descriptions then had to be typed and the maps and sketches drawn. We are grateful to Jack Edwards for writing the Foreword and to the Hertford Museum and Public Records Office County Hall for permission to reproduce illustrations.

While every care has been taken in the description of the walks it should be appreciated that the countryside is constantly changing and in the course of time some rights of way can become overgrown or otherwise obstructed. Should you encounter these or other problems, please let us know by writing to our publishers, Castlemead Publications, Swains Mill, 4A Crane Mead, Ware, Herts., SG12 9PY.

The East Herts Footpath Society has a full programme of walks throughout the year, organises rights of way clearances each month and various other activities. The annual membership subscription is £2 per household (50p for the unwaged). If you would like to know more about the Society, publicity material can usually be found in tourist offices and the larger public libraries in East Hertfordshire. In case of difficulty please write to the Membership Secretary, 4 Quaker Road, Ware, Herts.

CONTENTS

Queen Hoo Hall (south view) — Buckler 1832

COUNTRY CODE

Enjoy the countryside and respect its life and work

Guard against all risk of fire

Fasten all gates

Keep your dogs under close control

Keep to public paths across farmland

Use gates and stiles to cross fences, hedges and walls

Leave livestock, crops and machinery alone

Take your litter home

Help to keep all water clean

Protect wildlife, plants and trees

Take special care on country roads

Make no unnecessary noise

LANDOWNERS OBLIGATIONS

A person may not legally obstruct rights of way or make them more difficult to use or less easily followed. Generally an obstruction is anything which makes a right of way less commodious for public passage.

It is illegal to put barbed wire across a right of way. Even within the structure of a stile or gate the barbed wire may not cross a right of way, but should terminate on either side of the fixture.

A farmer may plough the surface of a path or bridleway, provided that he reinstates it within 14 days. But owners or tenants may not plough or remove the surface of a 'Road used as a Public Path' or a 'byway' or 'headland path' (ie. a path which goes round the edge of a field).

Further information can be obtained in the free pamphlet 'Rights of Way' issued by Hertfordshire County Council.

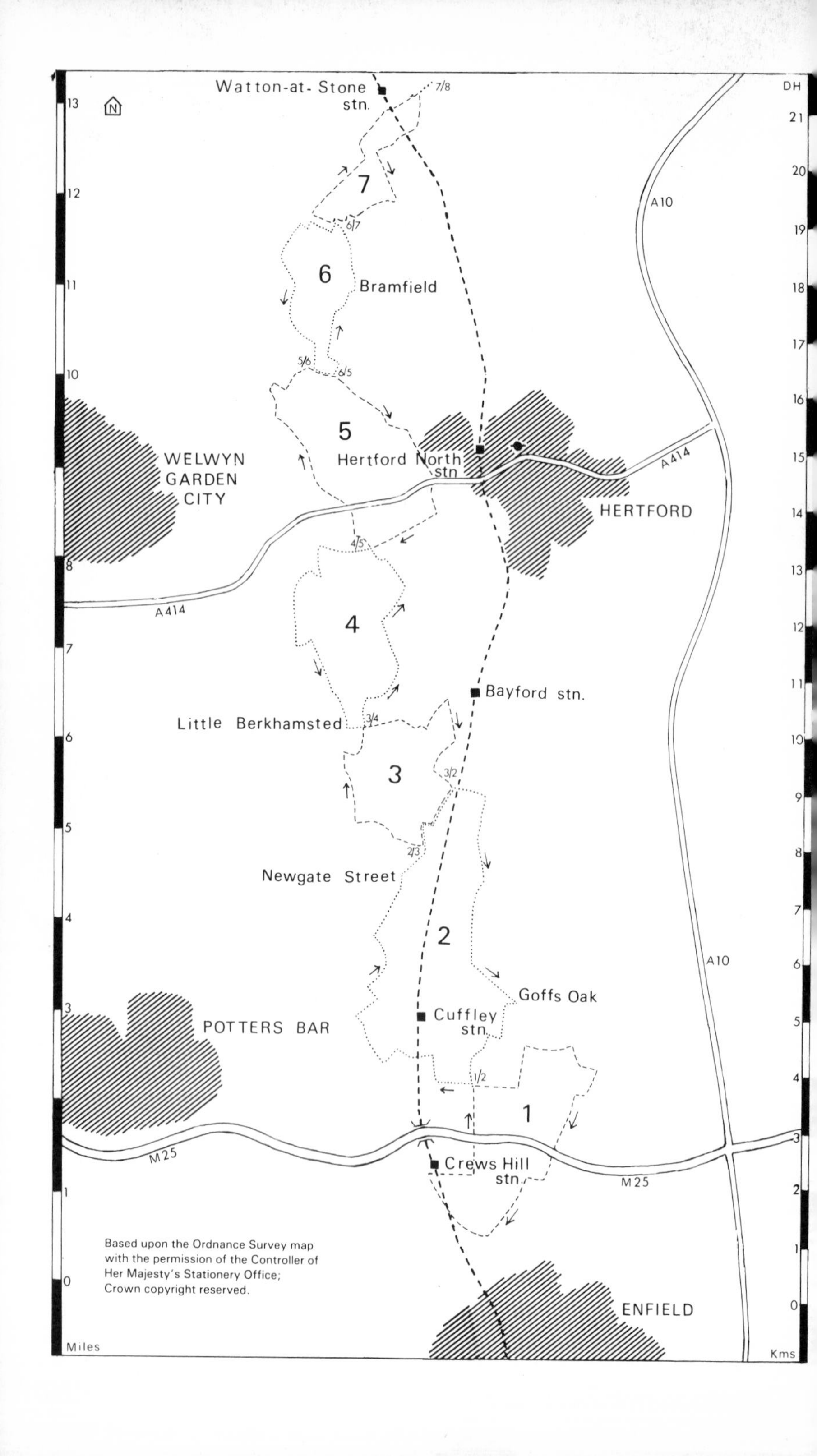
Watton-at-Stone stn.
7/8
DH
7
6/7
A10
6
Bramfield
5/6
6/5
5
WELWYN GARDEN CITY
Hertford North stn
A414
HERTFORD
4/5
A414
4
Bayford stn.
Little Berkhamsted
3/4
3
3/2
2/3
Newgate Street
2
Goffs Oak
A10
POTTERS BAR
Cuffley stn.
1/2
1
M25
Crews Hill stn.
M25
ENFIELD
Miles
Kms
Based upon the Ordnance Survey map with the permission of the Controller of Her Majesty's Stationery Office; Crown copyright reserved.

ROYSTON
Ashwell
Stn.
15
Therfield
14
Sandon
13
12
Cottered
11
Moor Green
10
9
Haultwick
8
BALDOCK
STEVENAGE
BUNTINGFORD
A10
Watton - at - Stone stn.
Kms.
Miles
Based upon the Ordnance Survey map
with the permission of the Controller of
Her Majesty's Stationery Office;
Crown copyright reserved.

KEY TO SYMBOLS

Footpath (not always visible on ground)

Track

Road

Direction of walk

Watercourse

Hedge

Fence

Woodland

Pond

Bridge

Building, Church

Linking point

Starting point

WALK NO. 1

Whitewebbs Park to Crews Hill

Whitewebbs Park – Crews Hill – Woodgreen Farm – Broadfield Farm – Whitewebbs Park

Distance 7 miles

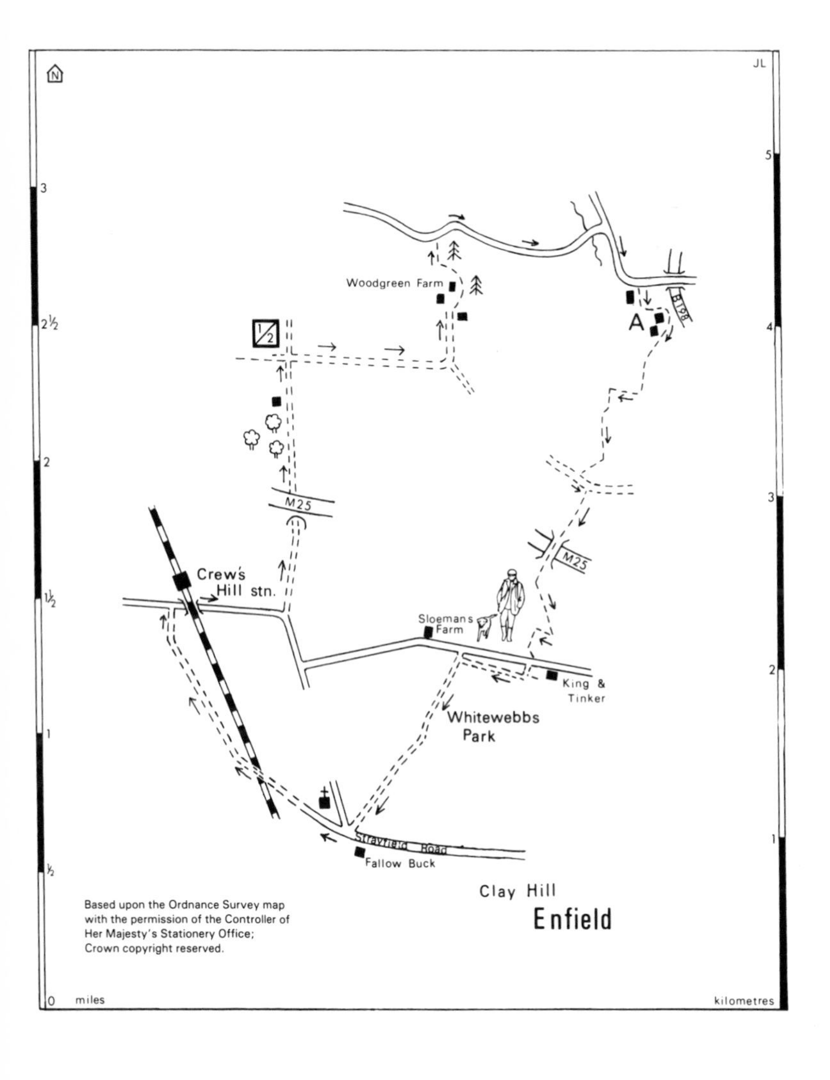

Park just west of the 'King and Tinker' public house alongside fence of Whitewebbs Park (GR 329998). Crews Hill (BR) Station is just over a mile from this point and is on the route of this walk.

This walk starts in Whitewebbs Road, alongside the boundary fence of Whitewebbs Park, about 100 yards west of the King and Tinker public house.

We now describe the route along the road because Whitewebbs Park is not always open. A route through the Park is preferable and you could proceed inside the Park along a bridlepath that runs parallel to the road. Go along the road for half a mile passing two entrances to Whitewebbs Park on your left. Turn left along a bridleway. Make this left turn before you reach Sloemans Farm which you can see to your right. This is a wide bridleway through the Park but it is usually muddy. You may prefer to use the path in the Park just beyond the fence on your left. Continue downhill until you cross a stream then proceed uphill. Further on uphill the bridleway becomes narrower. Keep straight on until you reach the road where you emerge opposite the Fallow Buck public house. Cross the road and fork right to proceed along Strayfield Road (a 'No Through Road'), passing the church on your right.

Walk northwestwards along Strayfield Road. You pass Astley House on your right. Keep straight on where the road becomes a gravel track at the Enfield Borough 'No Vehicles' sign. Keep straight on through a gateway and the path goes gradually uphill. Continue on through a kissing gate and along a narrow path with railings on both sides. Go downhill to cross the railway and then uphill on the path on the other side.

Straight on at the remains of a kissing gate through a wooded section. Continue on where another track crosses. You have woods on the right and a golf course on the left. Straight on along a grassy track where you have the golf course on both sides. Remain on this track and eventually it bears a little to the right and you continue on the track as you approach the club house. At the club house bear slightly right and cross the car park to emerge on to the road. There, cross to the far side and turn right on to the pavement and pass under the bridge at Crews Hill (BR) Station.

Continue with garden centres on both sides and, shortly after the Plough public house, where the road turns sharply right, you turn left into a lane with a board advertising 'Glasgow Stud', which you follow under the M25. Further along you cross a stile just before a quaint cottage on your left. You proceed slightly uphill until you come to a junction of tracks **1/2** and there you turn right passing Theobalds Park Estate sign on your left.

You are now on a wide gravel lane. The lane goes over a rise and crosses a large ditch and then continues uphill. When you reach the junction of tracks turn left. You pass under electricity wires close to a pole on your left which carries wires going in three directions. This is a

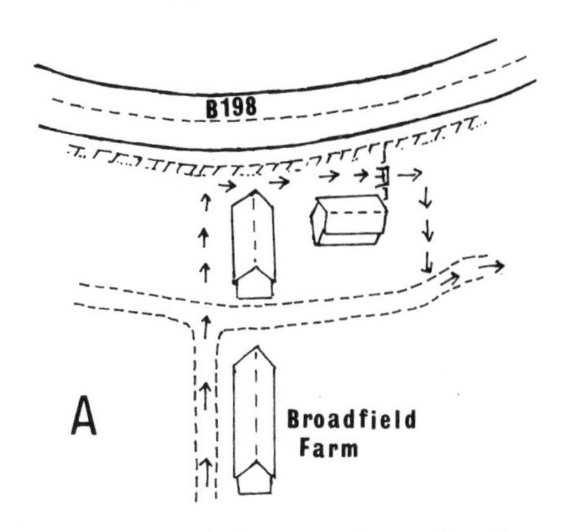

wide gravel track with a hedge on the left and field on the right. Pass under the electricity wires. Pass through a gateway and bear right at Woodgreen Farm. At a junction of tracks a few yards distant bear left and proceed between farm buildings. After the farm remain on the track, which has a couple of bends, until you reach the road and there turn right.

Continue on the road to the T-junction, where there is a letter box. Turn right. Pass a 'left bend' road sign. After the left bend, and after you pass the houses on your right, turn right along a footpath with the boundary of the house on your right. In approximately 200 yards, at the junction of tracks turn left. Pass under electricity wires. Pass a power pole on your left where the wires terminate. Proceed along a track where there are houses. Make a left and then a right bend to stay on the surfaced track. At the junction with the concrete track cross over and keep straight on. In a few yards, just before you reach the fence alongside the dual carriageway, turn right (*see* sketch A). In another few yards you climb over a stile beside an iron gate in front of you and turning right cross a grassy area to reach a gravel track and there turn left.

Pass through another gateway. You are going downhill walking directly away from farm buildings behind you and moving further away from the main road to your left. Take a wide wooden bridge over a ditch. Keep straight ahead to go through an iron gateway into a field and immediately turn right. In a few yards turn left, going uphill with the field on your left and the hedge on your right. The hedge peters out on your right but there is a line of trees. At the corner of the field cross a broken stile and immediately turn right so you continue with a hedge on your right and the field on your left. There are electricity wires in the field on your left.

At the corner of the field turn left and pass a power pole with double insulators on your right. You have a field on your left and a wood on your right. Where the wood on your right ends cross an earth bridge over a ditch and then turn right and continue with a field on your left and woods on your right. Where the wood ends turn right. You see houses on your left and you have to fork left before you reach the electricity wires. Pass under the electricity wires and pass close to old sheds and buildings on your left. You soon reach a gravel track and there turn left.

In about 75 yards you turn right at the signpost 'Public Footpath to Whitewebbs Road'. There is a 'Private No Footpath' sign. (The section of gravel track which you have just used is the only part that is a public right of way.)

You are on a grassy track with an open field on both sides and a view of London ahead. Cross the M25 on the concrete footbridge. Keep straight on along a grassy path which has fields on both sides. Pass under electricity wires with a pylon to your right. You are now leaving Hertfordshire and entering the London Borough of Enfield. Descend to a ditch which you cross, go over a stile and continue in the same direction with the field to your left and a hedge and fence on your right.

At the corner of the field cross the stile and turn right along a narrow path between hedges and fences. In just over 50 yards turn left along a path which is muddy and has fences on both sides and stay on this path until you emerge on to the road – Whitewebbs Lane – opposite the King and Tinker public house. (You will have to cross a sequence of stiles.) Turn right along Whitewebbs Road to return to the start of the walk.

The King and Tinker Inn — c.1884

WALK NO. 2

Goffs Oak to Newgate Street Village

Goffs Oak – Cuffley – Newgate Street Village – Wormley Wood – Goffs Oak

Distance 9½ miles

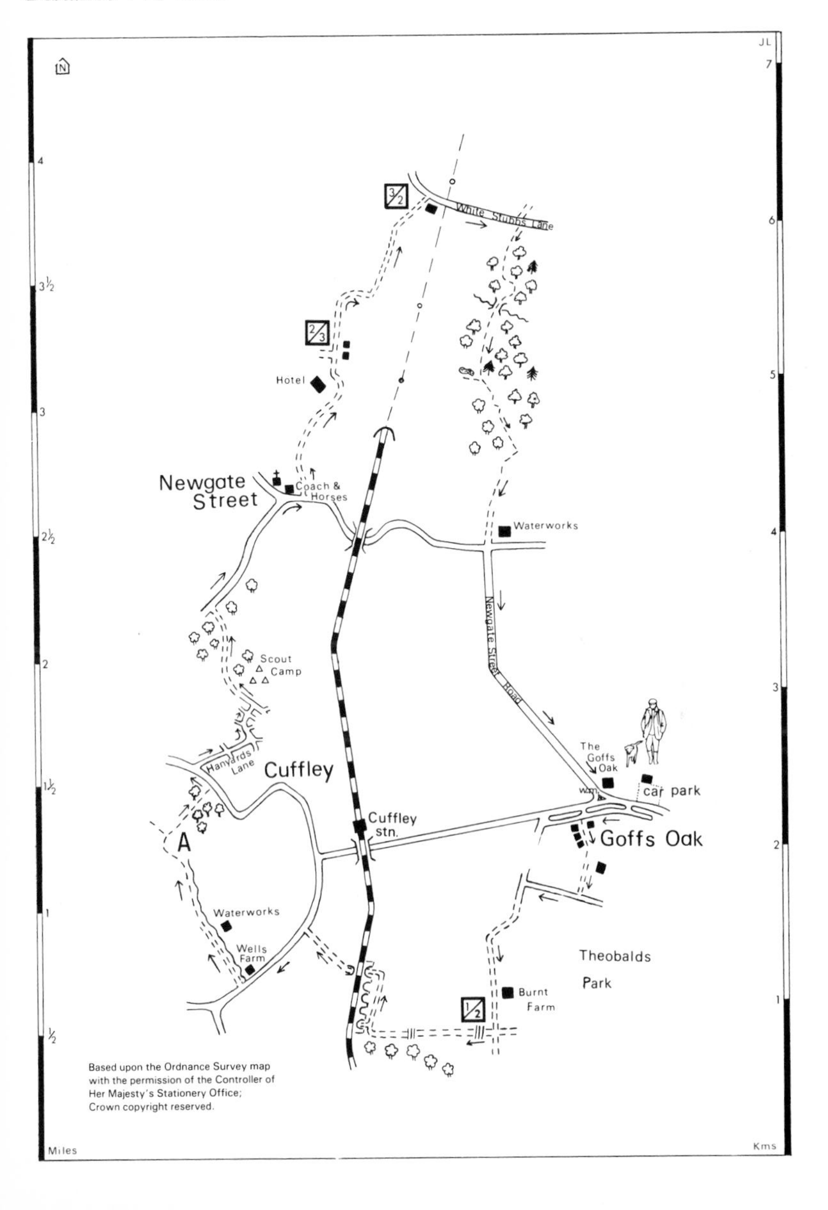

There is a public car park in front of Goffs Oak Library which is entered 100 yards to the east of the War Memorial, from Goffs Lane. A pedestrian right of way emerges alongside the Post Office which is a few paces from the War Memorial. Cuffley (BR) Station is 1 mile west of this point along Cuffley Hill.

This walk starts at the bottom of Newgatestreet Road, Goffs Oak, by the war memorial. Cross the main road and then turn right along the service road. Turn left at the footpath which is adjacent to house number 27. You will reach a bushy area. Keep left following a garden boundary fence on your left. The path becomes narrower and you have bushes or fences on both sides. You pass close to houses on your right, where there is a wooden garden fence, and on your left there is a hedge. Keep straight on through an area of brambles. Bear slightly left at a junction of grassy tracks where you have a big house further to your right. Proceed with a wooden fence on your right and another fence on your left. Next you have barbed wire on your right and a fence on your left. Keep straight on where there are wooden gates on both sides.

Cross a stile and proceed straight on uphill. Cross another stile to emerge on to a tarmac drive. Keep straight on and pass under electricity wires. At the junction with the road turn right. Keep straight on along the road ignoring stiles into the playing fields on your right. At the T-junction of roads turn left.

Good views here. Keep straight on where there is a gateway and the surface changes from tar to gravel. There is a notice here 'Theobalds Park Estate – Private – No Roadway'. Pass under electricity wires. The track goes down into a dip then up again, and at the brow of the hill you pass a farm on your left. Keep straight on until you reach a junction of tracks. [1/2] Ahead of you is a sign 'Private Footpath Only', and to the right is a cattle grid.

Turn right here to cross the cattle grid to continue on a gravel track with open fields on both sides. Keep straight on where the track goes downhill, and pass through a wide gap in a hedgerow. Continue on a level piece of gravel track with open fields on both sides. You reach another cattle grid that forms a bridge over a steam and there are woods close on your left. Go over the cattle grid and continue straight on with woods on your left and the railway viaduct ahead. Where the woods on your left cease turn right, to stay on the track as it curves to the right.

In 40 yards there is a junction of tracks. The main track makes a turn to the left but you continue straight ahead to cross a concrete bridge, walking parallel to the railway viaduct which you see to your left. The track goes uphill with open fields on both sides. In the middle of the field turn left where the track curves left. This turn is well before you reach the big pylon. You pass under electricity wires and at the edge of the field keep straight on to pass under the railway.

Keep straight on where the path has fields on both sides. Pass under

electricity wires. Keep straight on through a gateway and continue on a path with hedges on both sides until you pass through an iron gateway to emerge on to the main road. Turn left.

The road goes downhill and near the bottom you pass Wells Farm on the right. Cross a small bridge over a stream and then immediately turn right. Continue on a footpath where there is an open field on your left and a ditch on your right. This starts as a concrete track and then becomes a gravel track. Cross a stile alongside a gate and then continue straight on. Go through a gateway where you have a pair of houses and water works buildings on your right.

Keep straight on with an open field on your left and the ditch on your right. Go through another gateway and cross a concrete bridge over a ditch, pass under electricity wires and keep straight on. Stay on this muddy path as it curves to the left. Soon after that left bend there is an opening on the right where there is a broken footpath sign.

Make a sharp right turn there so that you continue with an open field on your left and a hedge on your right (*see* sketch A). As you proceed uphill look carefully for the point where the path enters the woods which are on your right. You may have the impression that this is a right turn, but the path is really straight on and it is the boundary of the woods which curves. Continue uphill on a fairly well defined path in a wooded area. Stay on this path which goes uphill and becomes narrower. The woods lie mainly to your left and you are close to the boundary on your right. Cross a stile to emerge on the road and turn left.

Turn right when you reach Hanyards Lane just before the '40 mph' speed-limit signs. Keep straight on where Bradgate joins on the left. Turn left at Hill Rise. Straight on at Woodview. Bear right where Warwick Avenue joins on the left. Straight on where Farm Close joins on the right. At the T-junction turn left.

Pass Tolmers Scout Camp entrance on your right and continue straight on along a lane. Where the lane ends keep straight on along a gravel path entering woodlands. Keep straight on uphill, ignoring a minor path on the left. Continue on this fairly well defined path through the woods, which has a wattle fence on the right-hand side until you reach the road and there turn right. The road goes steeply uphill and you continue until you reach Newgate Street Village and there turn right opposite the Coach and Horses public house.

In little more than 50 yards turn left on a public bridleway which is on the drive of Ponsbourne Hotel. The path has a tarred surface and goes downhill. The path rises again and you pass Ponsbourne Hotel car park on your left. Continue straight on along a gravel track. At the junction keep straight on, ignoring the path to the right. Veer slightly left, ignoring another path to the right. Pass tennis courts on your left, then, as the path veers left you pass silos on your right. The path then curves to the right and continues alongside a high, ornamental, brick wall.

Keep straight on, past a pair of cottages on your left and later, past houses on your right. 2/3 Straight on through a gateway on a gravel track with hedges on both sides. Where you have a power pole ahead turn right to stay on the track and pass under electricity wires. Pass a pond on your right and soon after that make a left turn to stay on the gravel track. Keep straight on until you pass a lodge and through a gateway to emerge on to a road. 3/2 Turn right. Pass under electricity wires. Pass a pair of houses on the right and continue along the road. Soon it curves at a point where there is a bridleway on the left and a footpath on the right. Turn right there across a stile on a path which leads to Darnacle Hill.

The path enters a wooded area going downhill and eventually goes down some steps and then you continue straight on uphill. Look for the yellow arrows on the trees which waymark the route. The path goes down another dip and you cross a stream on a plank bridge and continue up the other side.

The path curves to the right and then to the left to continue in approximately the same direction. It does another zig-zag right, turns left through a muddy area, goes more steeply downhill to cross a stream and then steeply up again on steps, and continues in the same direction through woods.

The path descends yet another dip, crosses a small stream on a plank bridge and goes up again. You reach an area which is more open where there is a ridge and there you must go straight on along a narrower path between bushes. The path takes a somewhat zig-zag route, generally veering towards the left. You gradually get closer to the woods which are to your left and when you eventually reach the edge of the wood turn right along a better defined path. This path is just inside the wood with the trees mainly to your left and to your right an area of bushes and general overgrowth. Keep straight on along this path.

When you come to an apparent junction of paths fork slightly right. It is in effect almost straight on. The main thing is not to stay on the wider track which turns left. You pass through a muddy area where there are old railway sleepers and continue straight on between bushes and small trees. At a minor junction fork left to stay on the main path. You reach a more open area where there is a junction of tracks and an old wooden gateway. Turn left to go through the gateway and enter a field and continue along the boundary hedge with the hedge on your left and the field on your right. The path goes through a scruffy area and you reach a gravel surface and then a gateway.

Go through the gate and continue along a gravel track. Pass under electricity wires. When you reach the roadway go straight on and pass water authority buildings on your left. At the road junction go straight on along Newgatestreet Road to return to the start of the walk.

Goffs Oak

WALK NO. 3

Bayford to Little Berkhamsted

Bayford – Tylers Causeway – Little Berkhamsted – Bayford

Distance 5½ miles

There is limited parking in the centre of this small village. Bayford (BR) Station is about half a mile away.

From the village take the road towards Brickendon. After passing The Baker Arms public house car park on your right, then take a track that

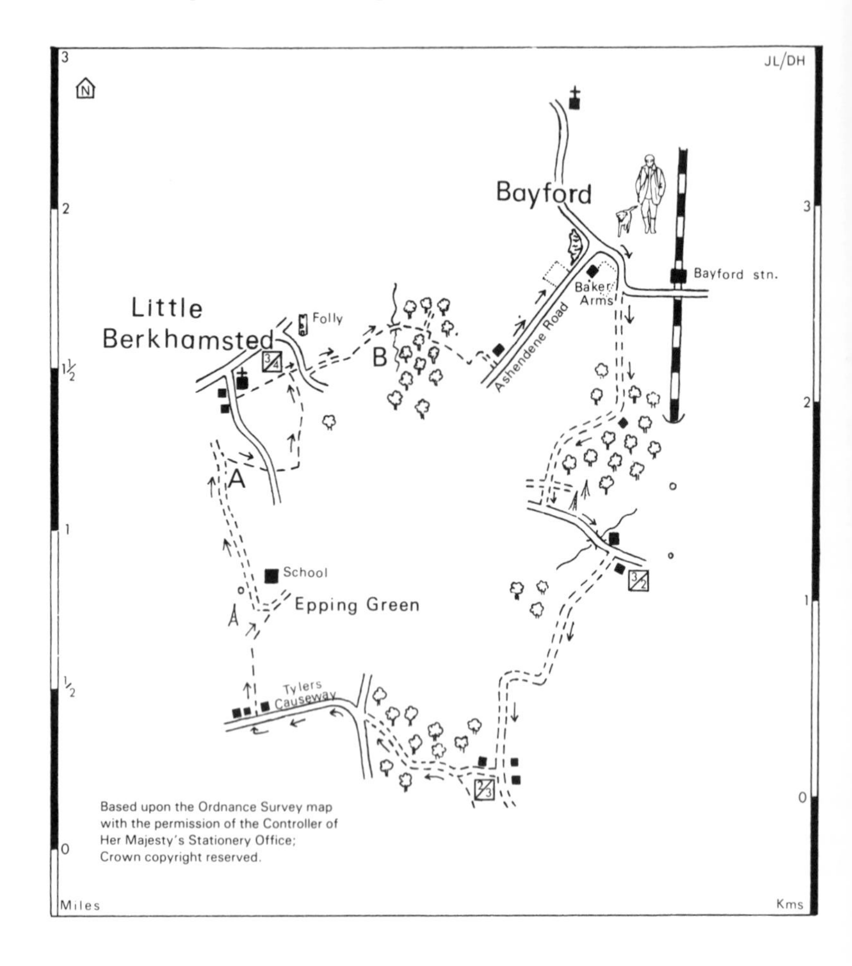

veers to the right into Blackfan Wood where you soon pass under power lines at right angles. Follow this wide track which first leads you into the middle of the wood, and then, just before a house, bends to the right and soon continues near the eastern edge of the wood. Ignoring another two wide tracks which branch off at right angles on your right you emerge from the wood opposite a garden centre and turn left along White Stubbs Lane.

When you pass a house on the left immediately turn right off the road, and pass a gatehouse on the left. 3/2 Continue along this tree-lined wide avenue which leads into Ponsbourne Park. Shortly before you come to a right-hand bend in the avenue circular ventilation shafts from the Ponsbourne railway tunnel can be seen protruding in the fields on the left. Pass through a gate across the track and continue past houses on the left built 1904–5. Just before the house on the right, turn right, 2/3 along a track which slopes downwards and bears right through woodland. Keep to the main winding track and emerge from the estate by a gatehouse on the right, dated 1879. Here you cross the road and continue along Tylers Causeway – the road opposite – which is signposted 'Essendon'.

About 50 yards past the large bungalow called The Willows turn right on to a concealed footpath to Little Berkhamsted; it is just before the garage of Tylers Cottage. Proceed over a stile at the edge of a field with the boundary on the the right and cross a second field via another stile, then go over a further stile into a third field and, still with the boundary on the right, head towards a large radio mast and water tower. After 170 yards turn right through the hedge (over a stile) and then immediately left inside a caravan site, with the boundary, which soon continues as a high brick wall, on the left.

Emerging on to a lane turn left towards the radio mast, and follow the lane, which turns right and passes the entrance to Epping House School and some houses. At the entrance to Woodcock Lodge continue past in the same direction along a wide gravel track until it turns right and here you turn left on to a wooded path which affords a good view to the west. This path brings you to a wooden gate (*see* sketch A). Pass through this and turn right. Cross the first field towards the stile and follow the same line across the second field, ending up at a second stile. When you cross this you go directly on to the road which could be dangerous for children jumping down.

Carefully cross the road and continue through the gate opposite in the same general direction, with the hedge on the right. The path turns left with the field boundary, to head towards the folly which is visible to the north. Continue until you reach the corner of the field, cross a stile on the right and turn immediately left, to continue in the same direction, passing through a short stretch of woodland. After a further two fields with the boundary now on the right, you come to the field's northern boundary opposite a bungalow, where you turn to the right. 3/4 After 20

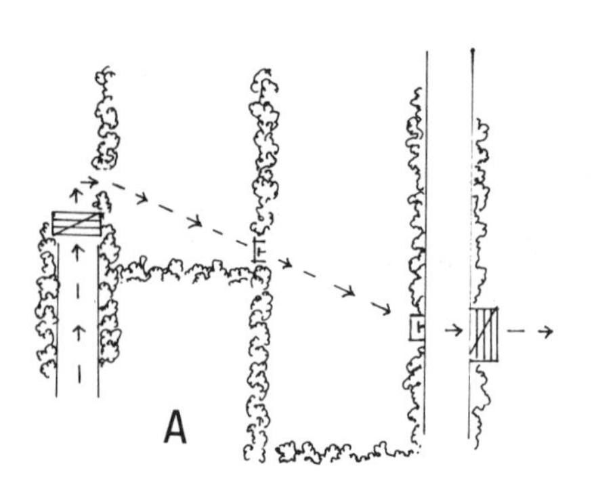

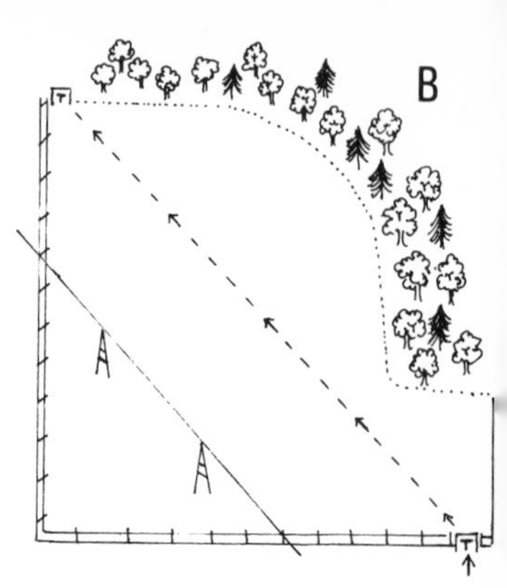

yards cross a stile and turn right along the road for 25 yards, then cross a stile on the left. Continue alongside Garden Cottage and then across the first small field, keeping to the hedge on the right. When you cross the next stile into the larger field, follow the path nearly parallel to the power lines, to enter the wood by crossing a stile and bridge near the corner of the field (*see* sketch B).

Continuing on the line of the bridge, follow the path through the woods, with barbed wire on your left. It turns right for a few paces and then continues left, in the same direction as before. Cross a drive at right angles and proceed as before, now with the wood on your right. You soon come out of the wood by crossing a stile and proceeding in the same direction, with the hedge on your left. Then, turning to the left, still alongside the hedge, cross a stile. This leads to a track which turns right to join Ashendene Road alongside two semi-detached houses beside Bayford House. Turning left follow the road for the last half mile back to the starting point in Bayford village.

The Five Horse Shoes, Little Berkhamsted — Whitwell 1892

WALK NO. 4

Little Berkhamsted to Letty Green

Little Berkhamsted – Water Hall – Letty Green – Little Berkhamsted

Distance 6 miles

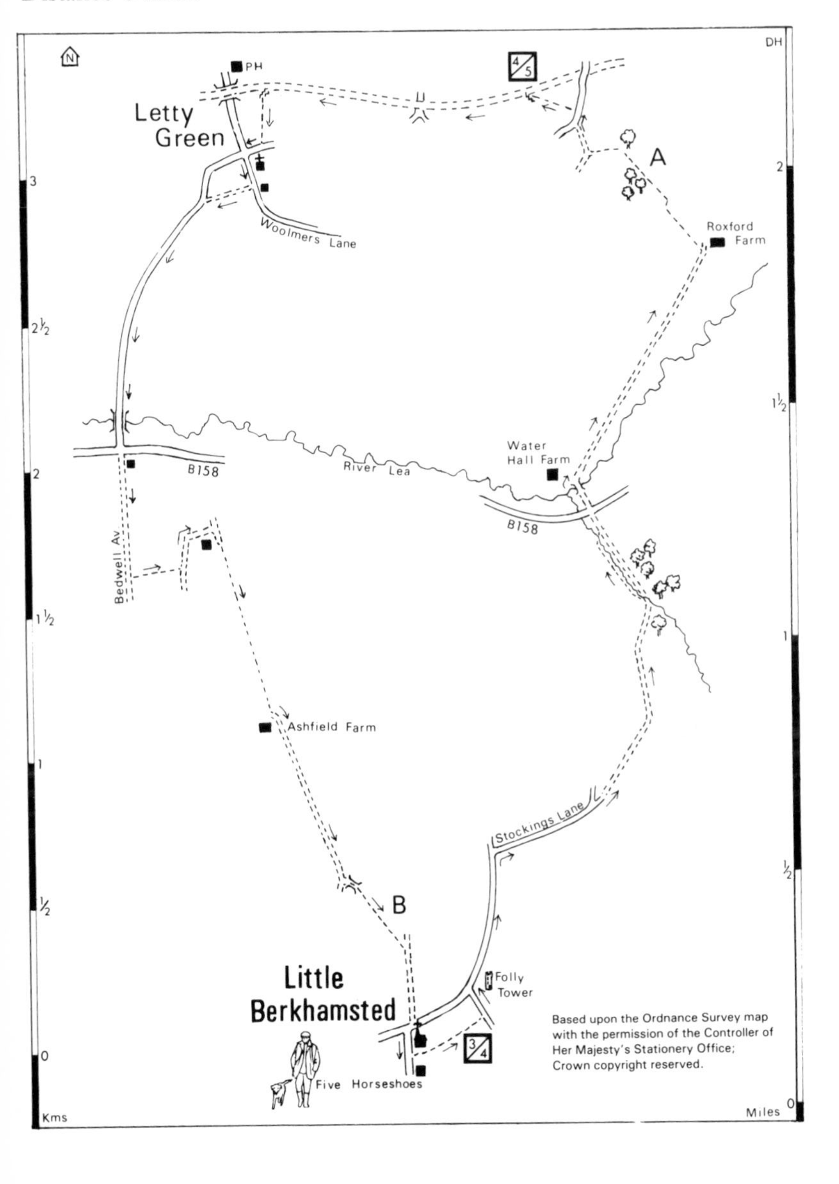

Parking is usually available outside the church or towards that end of the main road through the village.

Starting from the Five Horseshoes public house walk towards the church. Just before you reach it turn right over a stile by a signpost marked 'Public Footpath – Bayford 1½ miles'. You are now in a grassy meadow with the church on your left. Keep straight on, so that you have the hedge on your left, through the next field until you reach a stile. 3/4 Go over the stile on to the road with a brick wall opposite you, and turn left. Turn right at the next road junction. Use care on this road as there is no path on either side. Keep straight where there is a lodge on your right, but look across to the gate on your left, where you have views across Hatfield and Welwyn Garden City.

After the road traffic sign indicating a road junction turn right into Stockings Lane. This lane narrows and goes downhill. Where the lane bears left leave it and go straight on along the stony track in front of you. There is a signpost 'Public Footpath – Bayford ¾ miles'. The stoney track goes gradually downhill, with a barbed wire fence on your right and a hedge and trees on your left. In front of you you can see woods. When you reach some buildings bear to your right, so that you pass the red brick house on your left. There is a signpost indicating 'Bridleway – Water Hall'. Go straight along a very narrow path going downhill with hedges on either side. The path becomes darker with hedges closing above and is generally muddy underfoot. This path takes you to a footbridge over a river bed which is usually dried up.

The next part is difficult to describe.* At the bridge do not cross but immediately bear left, uphill, away from the river bed. At the top of this bank there is a barbed wire fence, cross into a field where you bear right, so that you walk along the edge of the field with the open field to your left and the general wooded area to your right. Near the end of the field bear right, where there is a concrete bridge which you cross, and then immediately bear left.

†You should now be on a track with hedges on either side. You pass some houses on your left and then emerge on to the B158 road; be careful here. Cross the road and enter the premises of Water Hall, a gravel quarry. You are on a tarmac road. Pass under the electricity wires with a double pole on your right, cross the river and turn immediately right. After you pass the water authority concrete bridge the river bends away to the right but you keep straight on along a wide gravel track with a hedge on your right. Pass a gravel 'lake' on your left 200 yards after the concrete bridge. The gravel operators may well have made some tracks to the left, but you must ignore them. Turn left when you reach

* We have described the official route which also happens to be the best, but you can cross over the bridge, turn left and follow the line of the riverbed crossing another wooden bridge and continuing beside the river bed to the concrete bridge. [Now rejoin the main text.]†

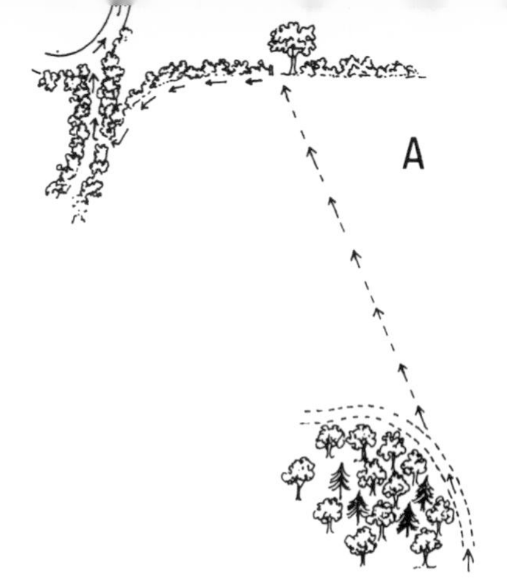

the farm buildings. Do not turn right where you see a white gate on your right-hand side, but continue straight up the track. There is a signpost and you follow the direction of the arm which says 'Footpath only', in other words, keep straight on. You are now going uphill with the hedge on your right and the field to your left. When you reach the corner of the field it is worth looking at the view behind you.

Turn right, cross over a stile and immediately turn left to continue in approximately the same direction as before. You are now going gradually uphill, with the woods on your left and the field on your right, and you come to the point where the wood on your left curves away. At the very start of that curve keep on going straight ahead into the field and leaving the edge of the woods (*see* sketch A). Walk straight across this large field, where the right of way is often not visible, aiming for a large solitary tree on the far side.

When you reach the tree, turn left along the edge of the field, with the hedge on your right. In 120 yards find a small gap in the hedge on your right. Turn right through the gap, and bear right, on to a track passing a small green stable on your right, until you emerge on to a bend in a lane. Turn right and in about 40 yards turn left off the lane through a gateway. Walk down a slight hill keeping the hedge and ditch about 8 yards distance on your right. Pass close to a power pole, bearing very slightly right to the corner of the field, and cross the ditch into the next field.

Continue in the same direction slightly downhill passing a large tree on your right. At the bottom of the field cross the plank bridge. Wild watercress grows here. Twenty yards ahead you see the steps to the disused railway track. Climb the steps and turn left to go along the course of the old railway. **4/5** Follow the railway track for a little over a half mile. This means you keep straight on where the first footpath crosses until you come to a stretch where there is wooden fencing and a picnic area on your right. Look for a flight of concrete steps on your left, opposite a gate on your right. Turn left there, going down the steps.

Proceed along this very narrow path until you emerge on to a road. Turn right. At the road junction, by the church, turn left along Woolmers Lane. About 250 yards along the road, opposite house number 8, turn right along a track. Follow the track, which has a small woodland on the left. When you reach the road turn left. In just over half a mile the road goes over the River Lea, and soon after that you come to a junction of roads where you cross the B158. Go straight on through the gates along Bedwell Avenue. Pass Hertford Lodge on your left on a wide bridleway. In a quarter mile look carefully for a left turn which is beside a paddock and leads up to a gate and a stile. When you have crossed the stile go uphill, across a large field, aiming for a big tree you can see on the horizon. Go over the gate by the big oak tree and turn left on to a gravel road passing a large white house on your left.

When you reach a small white bungalow, turn right on to a footpath signposted to Little Berkhampsted. In about 50 yards cross a stile and then proceed into a field where you have a hedge on your right and the field on your left. At the corner of the field cross the stile to enter another large field which you have to cross, maintaining the same direction. If the right of way is not visible, aim for a point well to the left of a white bungalow you see beyond the field boundary. As you cross the field you pass under electricity cables and gradually converge with the hedge on your left. Eventually the path runs alongside the hedge and you continue to the corner of the field where you cross a stile. In the next field continue in the same direction with a barbed-wire fence on your left-hand side. On reaching the corner of the field, cross the stile. You will probably notice the smell of the pig farm. Almost directly in front of you is a very muddy bridleway with hedges on each side.

Continue on this bridleway which means you maintain the same general direction. Keep straight on where a path joins on your left. Eventually you cross a concrete bridge with wooden fencing and then emerge into a large field. Sometimes the right of way here is not visible. You bear slightly left to cross the field diagonally, aiming for a gap in the left-hand hedge this side of the distant left-hand corner (*see* sketch B). You start on level ground and then go gradually uphill. There is a copse which you pass about 200 yards to your right and you gradually converge with the hedge on your left. Aim for the first gateway and pass through on to a track where you bear right. (Usually there are good views behind you on a clear day.) The track brings you to a road where you turn right. In a few yards turn left at the war memorial to reach the Five Horseshoes public house.

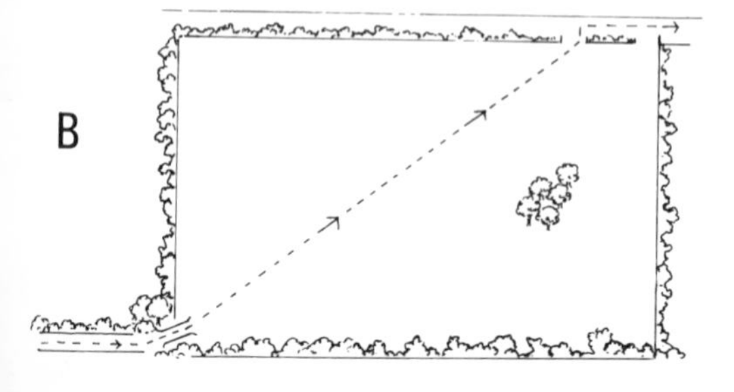

WALK NO. 5

Hertingfordbury to Marden Hill

Hertingfordbury – Birch Green – Marden Hill (near Tewin) – Hertingfordbury

Distance 6½ miles

Parking is easiest at the north end of the village on the cul-de-sac piece of the old road near the A414 roundabout. There is also space to park in St Mary's Lane near the church.

This walk starts from St Mary's Church, Hertingfordbury. Many of the paths used on this walk will be affected by new gravel pits and to some extent by the proposed Cole Green bypass. When these changes are made the East Herts Footpath Society will endeavour to get the diverted routes properly waymarked.

Walk south along the lane so that you leave St Mary's Church on your left-hand side. Pass under the bridge of the disused railway and turn left and immediately left again, climbing the bank on to the old railway. Turn left again, so that you are now on top of the bridge crossing the road and heading in a westerly direction along the route of the old railway. After about 1 mile deviate slightly to the right up an embankment,

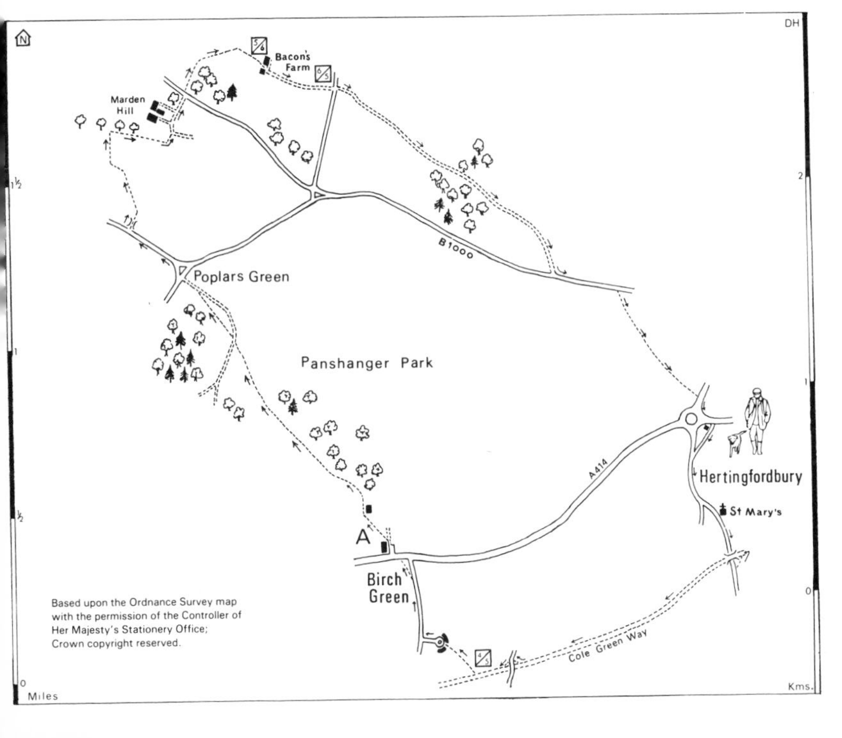

where you cross a lane (which leads to Staines Green), and down the embankment on the other side of the lane to rejoin the railway track. Continue for about 200 yards keeping a sharp lookout for a point where another path crosses; this is indicated by flights of steps on both sides of the track. 4/5 Turn right, go down the steps and across an open field towards some distant houses. When you reach the far side of the field, the path passes between the gardens of a row of houses and then a short tunnel takes you under the upper floors of the houses. When you emerge into a cul-de-sac continue straight ahead and when you reach the road junction turn right. You are now at Birch Green. As the construction of the Cole Green bypass may alter the features of this locality in the future, look out for new footpath signs.

It is best to use the footpath to the left of the lane to avoid walking in the roadway as you near the main road. Bear left across the green, passing the war memorial just to your right. When you reach the main road cross over and turn left, and walk about 50 yards along the pavement to a signpost marked 'Public Footpath – Poplars Green' beside a house. Turn right up a track which passes houses on your left. Just after the last house you reach the drive to Beechleight Farm, but instead of continuing up this drive enter the field on your left (*see* sketch A). With your back to the houses cross this rough field diagonally, aiming for the far left-hand corner.

At the corner of the field, cross a stile, pass between bushes and immediately swing round to the right. Pass through a gap to continue a few yards between bushes. When you emerge, there should be a rough area of field to your left and a boundary fence and hedge of a house to your right. After about 70 yards turn left, keeping to the boundary of the woods on your right with a pond to your left. (The pond may be filled in in due course.) Bear right and then left, following the boundary of the woods, and you will notice the path makes a dip at this point. Continue to follow the edge of the woodland which takes a zig-zag course. Eventually you will go down a slight incline, and then take a 90 degrees left turn up a slight incline. Keep close to the trees on your right and you will soon reach a part which is more open.

Bear right to cross the open area, where there is normally a grassy path between ferns. You will be going slightly downhill. (This part of the path, Hertingfordbury No. 10, may be diverted when more of Panshanger Park is opened up for gravel extraction.) Just beyond a point where a grassy track crosses you pass a notice to your right, 'Private Estate – No Admittance', and you bear left there to continue downhill and away from the notice. Cross a substantial stile and go straight on across the open field. Keep straight on where you have the boundary fence of a wood on your left to reach another stile. Cross that and bear slightly right to join a gravel track. Look up to the overhead power line and bear left, leaving the track to follow the route of the cables. The path passes between some bushes and then across an open area. Where

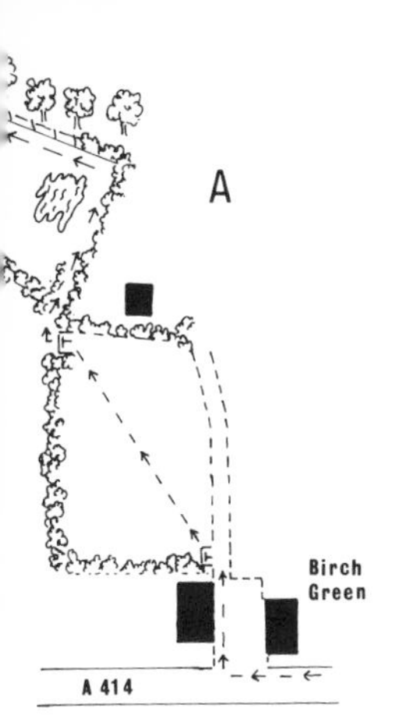

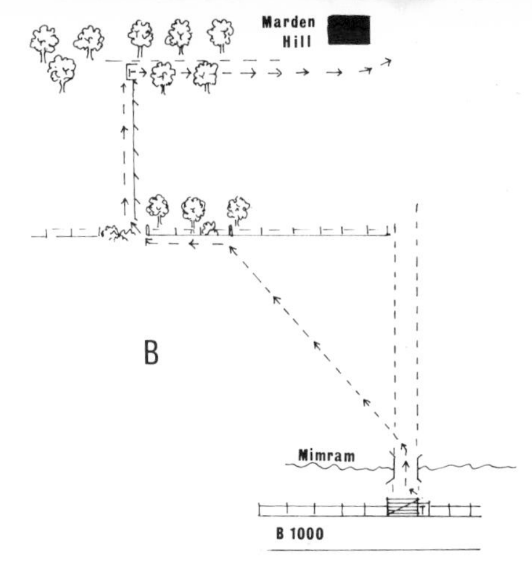

the power lines cease, keep straight on until you emerge on to a lane near the lodge. This is Poplars Green.

Cross the lane and keep straight on up a short section of road to the main road junction, signposted 'Welwyn B1000'. Cross over the B1000 carefully and turn left, walking along the road in the direction of Welwyn until you reach a stile by the side of a gate on your right signposted 'Public Footpath to Tewin'. Turn right off the road and, crossing the stile walk along a footpath with 'Private – Keep Out' signs on both sides. In a few yards you cross the river Mimram and keep straight on. You reach another stile, which you cross, then turn 40 degrees left, and continue diagonally across an open field, going gradually uphill. Looking to your left you will see farm buildings and, beyond them on the skyline, tall buildings in Welwyn Garden City (*see* sketch B).

When you reach the far side of the field turn left and follow the line of trees on your right. Look for a gap in the barbed wire fence on your right and turn right there. Do not go over the piece of wooden fence in front of you but immediately turn 30 degrees left, through the bushes, and emerge into a field with a wire fence on your right. Cross the field and, keeping the fence on your right, aim for a line of tall trees. (This path, Tewin No. 22, may be diverted when the land is opened up for gravel extractions.) When you reach the avenue of trees, turn sharp right, cross a stile and proceed along the avenue. Keep straight on where the avenue ends and pass in front of the big house, Marden Hill. Keep straight on, with railings on your left. When you reach the corner of the railings, turn left so that you continue with the railings on your left. You soon reach a gate and a broken stile. Cross the stile and follow the track ahead of you, cross the drive that leads to Marden Hill on your left and keep straight on. You have railings to your left, with buildings beyond and a fence and field on your right. Pass the entrance to Marden Cottage opposite and woodland on your left and emerge on to a road. Cross the road to the farm track, where there is a concealed signpost 'Public Bridleway to Hertford'.

Follow this track with an open field on your left and wood (Red Wood) on your right. Keep to this track close to the edge of the field as it curves right. You continue along a stretch which has a hedge on the right and the field on the left until you reach a stile and gate. Cross the stile and turn 45 degrees right, aiming for the stile and gate you can see on the far side of the field. Cross this stile and turn a little to your left to go along a track between farm buildings at Bacon's Farm. 5/6 Continue on a good gravel track between hedges. Keep straight on across a tarmac lane where there is a signpost 'Hertford Road 1 Mile'. 6/5 The track remains fairly well defined on the ground but as you get nearer to the woods it becomes narrower. Close to the woods there is a section where you have woodland on your right and the field on your left and soon after that you enter the woods.

Going through the wood try to maintain the same general direction, ignoring the tracks to the right. You pass through an area where the woods are thick on both sides but after that there is a section where you are close to the boundary of the wood on your left. This means that you are about 20 yards inside the wood. Keep close to the left-hand boundary and when you reach the end of the wood keep straight on along a path where there is a hedge on your left and an open field on your right.

When you reach the point where there is a small woodland in front of you, keep on the gravel track which turns right and goes downhill. You then go up a gradient and when you reach the road turn left and walk along the grass verge. Just before you reach the built-up area you will see a signpost 'Public Footpath – Hertingfordbury' on the right side of the road. Cross the road and enter the field; the path crosses the field diagonally to the left towards the woodland. (This path may be diverted when the area is opened up for gravel extraction.) When you reach the far side of the field enter the wood and continue in the same direction. The path then bears slightly left to follow the boundary of the woods and then emerges into an open area.

The path goes straight on across part of the open field with woods further away to your left. The boundary of the woods gradually converges again with the line of the path and there you continue with the edge of the woods close to your left. At the junction of tracks turn right along a piece of track, usually muddy, with fences on both sides. Look carefully for the place where the path turns diagonally left away from the track and turn left there. Do not go straight ahead downhill where there is a notice 'Private Estate – Keep Out'. Continue with woods on your right and the fence on your left. The path continues through the woods, going gradually downhill, and emerges on to a road. Cross carefully and turn right to the roundabout. Cross over the main road at a convenient point to the left of the roundabout and take the side road back to Hertingfordbury and St Mary's Church.

WALK NO. 6

Bramfield Woods going South

Bramfield Woods – Queen Hoo Hall – Bramfield Village – Bramfield Woods

Distance 4½ miles

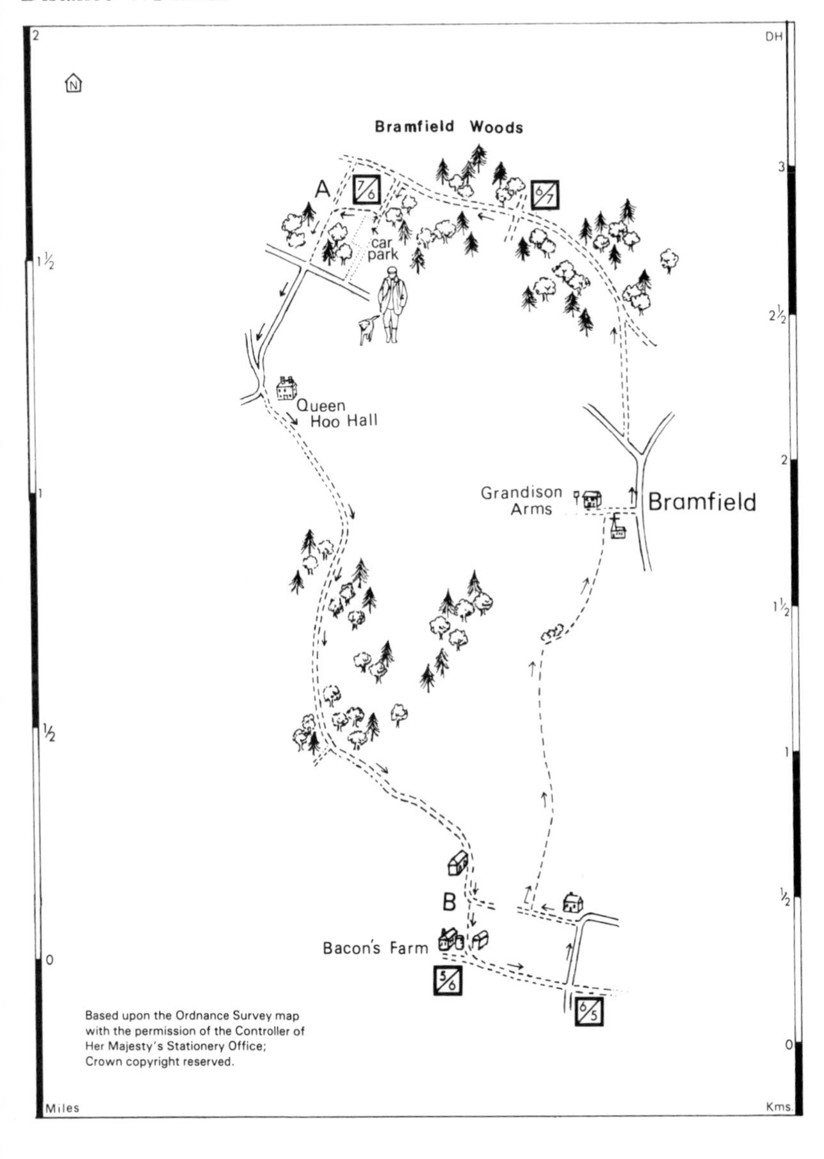

Easiest parking is in the Forestry Commission car park which is just off the north-eastern side of the Datchworth road, 1 mile from Bramfield (GR 283166). (This is the same starting point as walk No. 7 – Bramfield going North.)

This walk starts from the Forestry Commission Car Park 1 mile north-west of Bramfield on the Bramfield to Datchworth Road.

Walk north from the car park passing through a gate and by the Forestry Commission sign. **7/6** Immediately turn left and follow a not very distinct path through the woods which goes at right angles to the line of the car park (*see* sketch A). (Ignore a minor path bearing left.) The path that you are on goes downhill, bending a few times between the trees. Cross a small ditch at a dip in the path, at the fork after the ditch bear left and in about 25 yards you will emerge on to a gravel track. There turn left going downhill. When you reach the road, cross it, and continue along the lane signposted 'Tewin 1 mile' along Tewin Hill. Keep straight on where Queen Hoo Lane joins on your right.

At the bend in the lane walk straight on, along a track signposted 'Public Bridleway to Tewin 1 mile'. (To your left is Queen Hoo Hall.) This is a gravel track with bushes on both sides. You reach a wooden gate and you maintain the same general direction going downhill along the track. There are open fields on both sides and a good view ahead. The track veers slightly to the right but generally maintains the same direction. The ground levels out as you get closer to Bramfield Park Wood ahead of you and the track bears to the right a little just before it enters the woods. (It can be very muddy here.)

Keep straight on at a very muddy section where another track crosses and you will see a Forestry Commission sign on your left. Ignore this sign and keep straight ahead through the wood where it can still be extremely muddy. Where the path appears to fork, by a rustic fence towards open fields, continue walking straight ahead along the track, so that you are just inside the wood. This section is very muddy indeed and you may find firmer routes through the bushes on either side. Through the bushes to your right you should see an open field. Eventually you start going uphill again on a muddy section.

Before leaving the wood you see a path joining you on your right, and you should walk ahead to the left, slightly outside the wood, with the field to your right and the woods to your left (*see* sketch B). About 100 yards beyond the wood boundary you fork right across an open field. The track is usually visible. There are good views here.

Looking across the field you can see the brown buildings of Westend Farm with a long roof. Aim just to the left of those buildings. You are now going gradually downhill, with a large field on both sides. Nearer to the buildings a hedge and ditch on your left gradually converge with the path. At the old buildings turn slightly right, to pass them on your right.

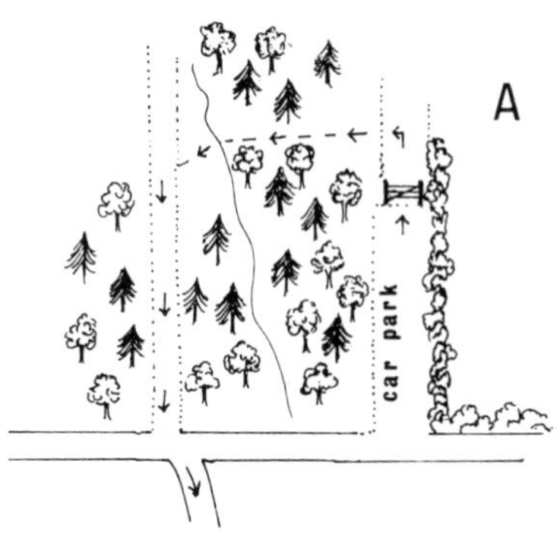

Ignoring the bridleway going off left, you soon come to a junction where a track joins from the right. There you turn left and almost immediately turn right to stay on the track. You have open fields on both sides. Soon the track turns left and there you leave it to go straight on (*see* sketch B).

You pass through a small group of young trees to find a broken stile in the hedge ahead. Cross the stile and go straight on across the field. You see Bacons Farm ahead to your right. Aim for the big tree straight ahead and eventually pass it on your right with the grounds of the farmhouse beyond to your right and a field on your left. You pass between farm buildings to reach another track where you turn left. **5/6** You then pass under electricity wires keeping a power pole to your left. This gravel track soon has banks and bushes on both sides. Where the gravel track crosses a lane turn left along this lane. **6/5** You pass under electricity wires with a power pole to your left. Just before the sharp right bend in the lane, turn left on to the gravel track passing in front of Westend House.

You are now on a gravel track with bushes on both sides. You pass under electricity wires and soon afterwards reach a point where the track takes a slight bend to the right and then to the left. Just as it takes the bend to the left you will see a double power pole to your right. Turn right and aim straight for the double pole and you may notice the remains of a hedge and ditch on your right as you proceed. Pass close to the double pole on your right and follow the line of the overhead wires straight ahead of you.

Continue straight on where a track crosses just before a power pole. At the sixth pole, which has double insulators, the wires fork further to the right but here you must keep straight on for just over 150 yards.

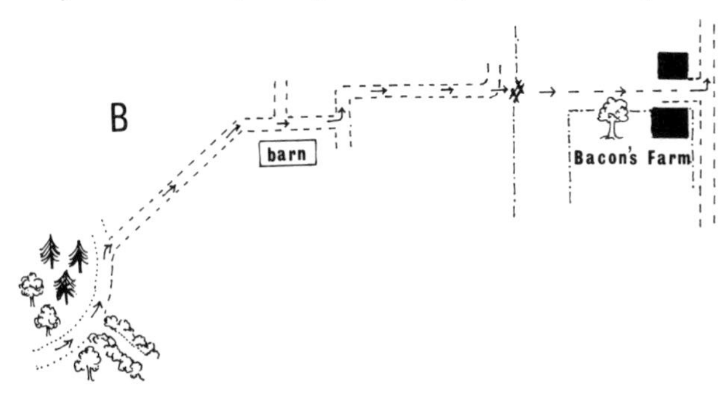

The wires are now further away to your right. Turn right and you may find the remains of a section of hedge on your left as you proceed. Seventy yards brings you to a power pole, where you are once again under the wires and there turn left. You go downhill with open fields on both sides, keeping the wires a little to your left. Ahead you see the spire of Bramfield Church.

At the bottom of the dip cross a stile after an earth bridge a little to the right and then continue uphill. Aim towards a stile by a large tree which appears to the right of the church spire. Pass the big tree to your right and continue straight, entering a sports field.

Continue along the right-hand edge of the sports field and you pass a kissing gate on your right, which is the entrance to Bramfield churchyard. (If you wish you can turn right there and then turn left at the main road on the far side.) Continuing straight on along the edge of the sports field, you pass some swings on your left and you see the Grandison Arms public house ahead. At the road turn right, and at the next road junction turn left along the main road. Keep straight on along the main road and continue straight on at the road junction where the main road bears very slightly left, signposted 'Datchworth 2½ miles'.

About 140 yards after the road junction fork right, going off the road, following a 'Public Footpath' sign. You go gradually uphill on a gravel track towards Brights Hill. There are bushes on both sides. You pass under electricity wires close to a pole on your right. A very muddy section here. Continue on the track uphill. You may find drier routes on the right-hand bank, but keep away from the edge of an old chalk pit. Keep straight on at the wooden gate. The path continues uphill into Bramfield Woods.

Keep straight on the main path, ignoring minor paths going off to the right. The path levels out and veers to the left. Keep straight on down into a dip where another path joins on your right. Go uphill to reach a gravel track and proceed straight across this. 6/7 Then to your left you will see a Forestry Commission 'No Riding' sign. You are now on a very wide grassy path. You come to a very muddy section and the path veers marginally to the right. You eventually cross a wooden barrier to reach a gravel track and then turn left. You soon pass a Forestry Commission 'No Riding' sign on your left. Keep straight on where a track joins on your left and continue on to the car park where you started the walk.

WALK NO. 7

Bramfield Woods going North

Bramfield Woods – Perrywood Farm – Watton-at-Stone – Gobions Farm – Bramfield Woods

Distance 4½ miles

Easiest parking is in the Forestry Commission car park which is just off the north-eastern side of the Datchworth road, one mile from Bramfield (GR 283166). (This is the same starting point as Walk No. 6 – Bramfield going South.)

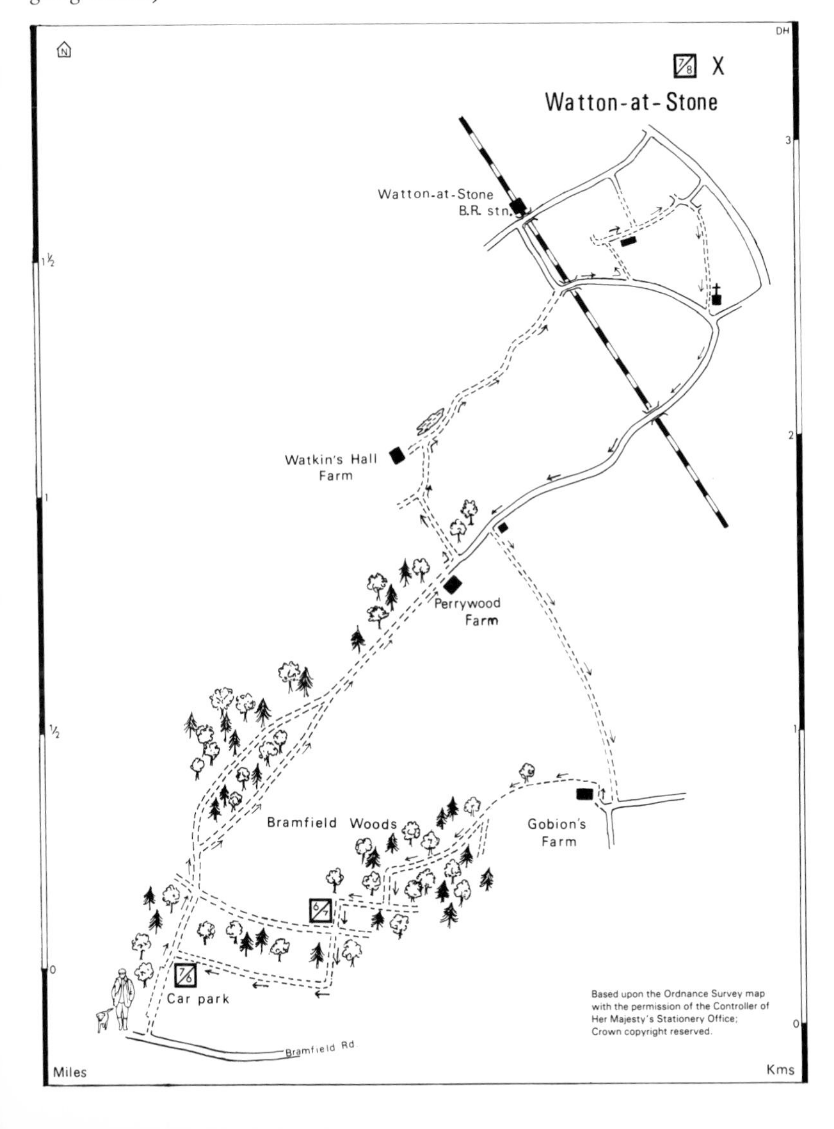

Walk away from the road through the wooden gate where there is a Forestry Commission sign. 7/6 Continue on a wide gravel track with woods on your left. Keep straight on where a track joins on your right and again when you cross a wide track.

When you reach a junction of tracks the definitive route goes straight on but a better path is the right fork along the edge of the wood (Long Walk, Perrywood Lane), so that you have the woods on your left and the field on your right. There is quite a good view from here. Keep on the downhill track with woods on your left, passing a path to your left, and eventually on your left you pass a junction with the definitive route, and if you look back you will see the Forestry Commission sign there.

Soon after that you reach a section of the track which has fields on each side. Continue straight on where you have hedgerows on each side and you will see in the distance farm buildings of Perrywood Farm.

Pass through the farm with buildings on your right and a few yards after that turn left where there is a bridleway sign. The bridleway starts off as a muddy track between bushes and then becomes a gravel track with open fields on each side. You will be heading towards Watkins Hall Farm. Pass through an iron gate and then bear right, keeping on the gravel track so that you pass the buildings of Watkins Hall Farm on your left. At the junction of tracks opposite Watkins Hall turn right along a surfaced lane (towards Watkins Spring North). You should see two ponds, one just before the right turn and one soon after. Both will be on your left. You soon pass through a gateway with a cattle grid and you keep straight on along a lane. Keep straight on where you have a house and bridleway sign on your right.

At the junction of lanes keep straight on, crossing the bridge over the railway. When the lane reaches a wooded area turn left, along a path which has a chainlinked fence on the left and a hedge on the right. The hedge is the boundary of a school playing-field. At the T-junction of paths turn right so that you still have the school on your right. When you reach the roadway turn right, and in a few yards turn left, along a surfaced path which has hedges and houses on each side. Keep straight on where a path joins on the left.

You reach a part where there is a playing field and sports pavilion on your right and a low brick wall runs alongside the path. Here the path gradually curves to your right. 7/8* At the point where there are swings on the right, turn right along a narrower path, so keeping the swings to your right and houses on your left.

(At this point you are in Watton-at-Stone and if you wish to get to the main road do not make the right turn by the swings, but keep straight along the wide path.)

The narrow path brings you to the church, where the path chicanes, keeping outside the churchyard, and soon brings you to a lane where

* There is no actual link point with Walk No. 8 which passes a short distance away.

you turn left. (You can if you wish go through the churchyard and emerge on the other side.) The lane goes downhill for a short distance with the church on your left. You then approach a T-junction of lanes, where you turn right. You are now going uphill directly away from the church towards Watton Green. Carry straight on up the hill where a path joins on your left. Continue along this lane going downhill, crossing the bridge over the railway. Keep going for quite a long distance downhill and then uphill until you pass a point where a footpath joins on your right and soon after that you pass a house on your left.

This is the first house after the railway bridge. At this point, where there is a signpost 'Bridleway – Stapleford 1½ miles', you turn left.

You keep straight on along this bridleway, which has open fields and good views on the left. After about two-thirds of a mile you reach a metalled lane at a T-junction and turn right. Very soon, where the lane does a left bend, bear right to pass through Gobions Farm. You pass close to the farmhouse on your right, keeping the farm buildings on your left. When you reach the field beyond the farm buildings turn left, so that you continue with the field on your right and new farm buildings on your left. After you reach the end of the grey farm building continue along the side of the field until you reach the corner. When you reach the boundary of the field, facing you will be a wood, where you turn left, to cross a fairly deep ditch, and then immediately right, to continue in the same direction, with the trees on your right.

About a hundred yards from the ditch you bear right, to enter the wood. Soon after entering the wood you meet a junction of tracks, where there is a Forestry Commission sign. Take the right fork. Where the track makes a left bend follow it and then turn right at the T-junction of tracks.

You should now be on a track with a firm gravel surface. At the junction of tracks bear left to continue along the gravel surface, keep straight on where a wide grass track crosses. 6/7 Where the gravel track makes a right turn follow it, and at this point you should see beyond the woods open countryside to your left. Stay on the gravel track until you reach a T-junction of tracks and there you turn left to return to the car park.

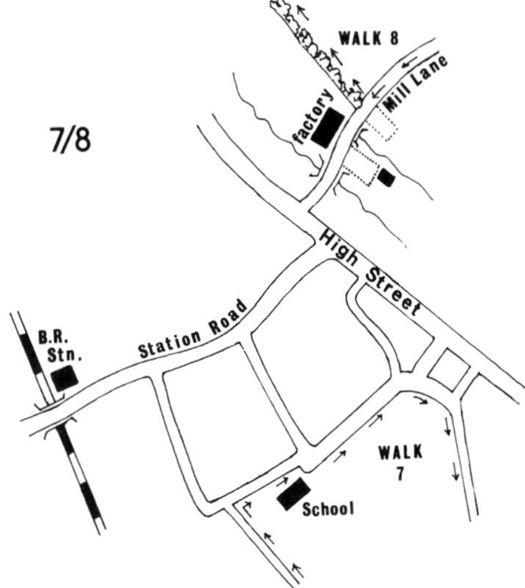

WALK NO. 8

Watton-at-Stone going North

Watton-at-Stone – Burn's Green – Hebing End – Gregory's Farm – Watton-at-Stone

Distance 7 miles

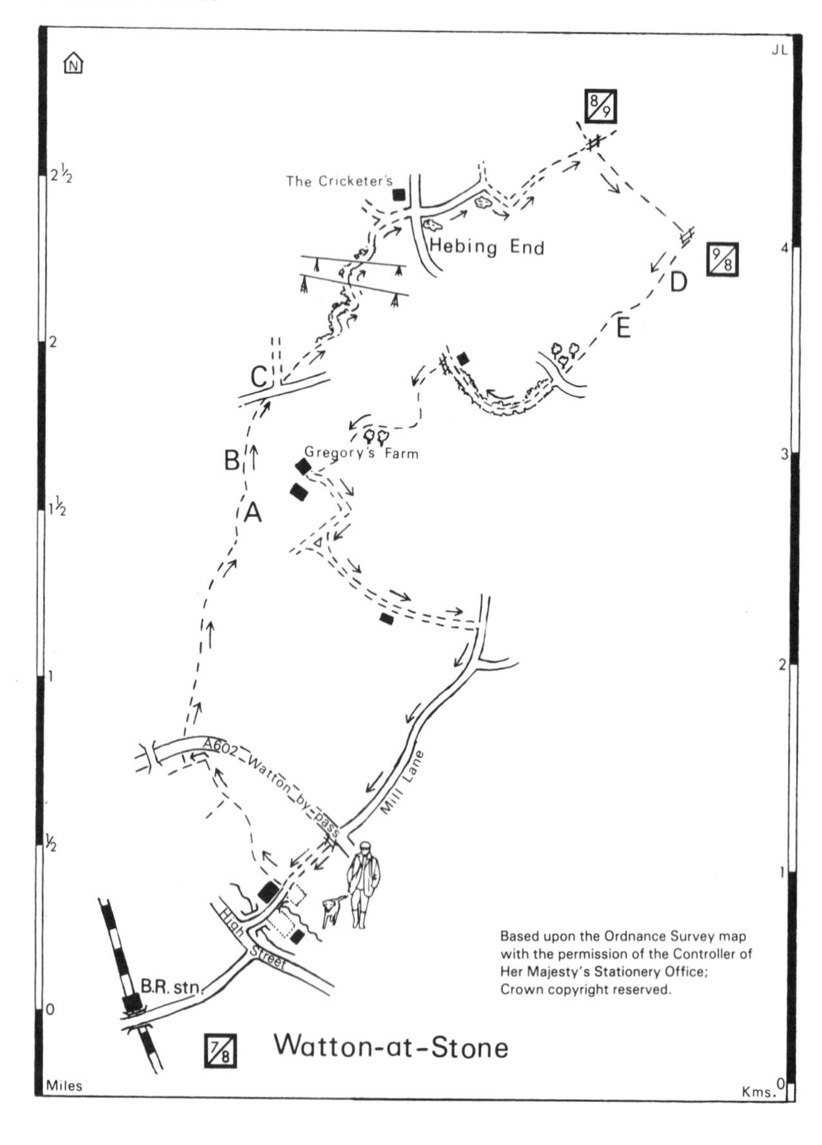

There are several roads in the village where cars can be left. Mill Lane at GR 300194 is a cul-de-sac where there is usually room to park.

Watton-at-Stone lies between Hertford and Stevenage a little to the west of the new bypass on the A602; it can also be reached by rail. An alternative starting point is from the Cricketers public house at Benington.

The description begins at Mill Lane, which lies on the east side of Watton High Street, a little north of where Station Road joins on the opposite side of the street. 7/8* Cross the bridge over the stream and just past the factory on your left you should see a signpost 'Public Bridleway – Benington 2½ miles'. Turn left here and continue along the edge of the field with the hedge on your left and the field on your right. Where the hedge ends and a track joins on your left continue on, bearing slightly to the right, to follow the line of a fence as you proceed. You pass close to a pair of large trees beyond the fence to your left and as you near the Watton bypass you reach another hedgerow. Soon after turn left, alongside the road on to a path between hedges, and continue 70 yards downhill. A few yards before the bottom of the dip, at a point where there is a small ditch or stream, turn right and emerge beside the bypass (A602).

Cross over the road with care, into the field directly opposite, following the line of the ditch, with trees and a hedge to your left and the open field on your right. Continue with the ditch on your left for a little more than a quarter mile, keeping straight on where a concrete farm track crosses. Later, you come to a waymark post by an earth bridge, ignore this and go ahead until you reach a point where the ditch on your left ends. Here bear very slightly left and cross the open field, which is usually ploughed or has a crop on it (*see* sketch A). You gradually converge with a hedge on your left, at a point where a short ridge runs at right angles to the hedge. Here turn left through the gap in the hedge.

Immediately after passing through the hedge turn right, so that you continue with the hedge on your right, following the curve of the hedge as it bears to the left, and continue in this same direction from where the hedge ends, so that you cross the open field diagonally (*see* sketch B). This is a large field and you are in the lowest part of a small dip. The field rises a little to your left and there is a small hill to your right. On the distant horizon you will see some woods. Between you and the

* See sketch at end of preceding walk.

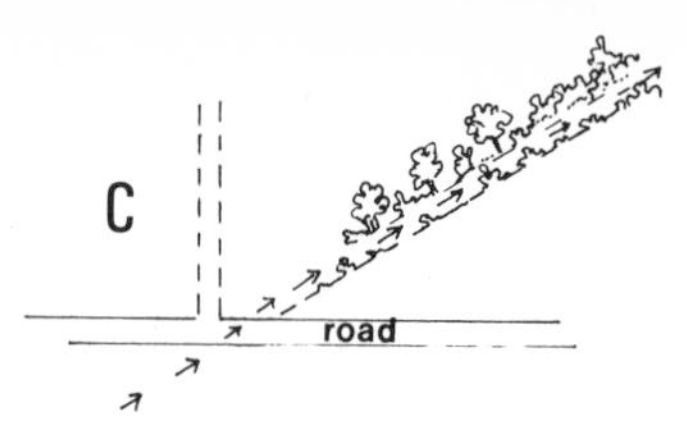

woods, at a low point, there are the remains of an old footpath signpost, which you may just be able to see. This is the point you are aiming for.

As you cross the field you come to a small bank. On the road over to your left, you may see a new footpath signpost. Do not turn towards it but continue across the bank in the original direction to the broken sign.

You should emerge on to the road at a point where a farm track joins on the other side. Do not take this track, which leaves the road at right angles, but use the less obvious path, proceeding in almost the same direction you were travelling in across the previous field (*see* sketch C). At first you follow the line of a ditch bordered by some scrubby bushes, then along a very narrow path between hedges. Gradually the path improves and becomes a firm wide path. Later there is a section which is always wet because of drainage from adjoining fields. Pass a pond on your left and bear right where the path curves, continuing through a muddy section and passing under two sets of overhead wires before emerging on to a lane. Bear right along the lane, continue past the houses and you will arrive at a road junction beside the Cricketers public house.

Cross over the road and walk straight down the lane opposite, which is signposted 'Hebing End'. At the far end of this lane is a pond and just beyond that you should see a 'Public Bridleway' sign. Turn right along this bridleway, walking with a fence on your left-hand side. Bear left, following the track and continue with a barbed wire fence to your left. You go gradually downhill and at the point where the track takes a right-hand bend you keep straight on, down the hill, with trees and hedges on your left.

At the bottom of the hill you pass through the hedge on your left, then continue in the same direction as before, with the hedge now on your right. Just before you reach a concrete bridge over a stream you will see a wooden gate on your right. 8/9 Turn right through this gate into a field. (There is often quite deep mud at this point, so take care.) Cross the stream at the first convenient point and continue down the middle of this narrow field keeping approximately 30 yards from the hedge on your left. When you reach the end of the field you should see an iron gate in the corner to your left. 9/8

The official right of way, which follows the field boundary to your right, is currently obstructed. We therefore suggest that you go through the gateway and follow a route on the further side of the fence (*see* sketch D). Cross the ditch (the Old Bourne) using the concrete bridge and turn right, following the ditch on your right until you reach a point where the ditch makes a left turn. Here you cross the ditch and continue straight ahead beside a hedge. (Alternatively, if the ditch is dry it is possible to

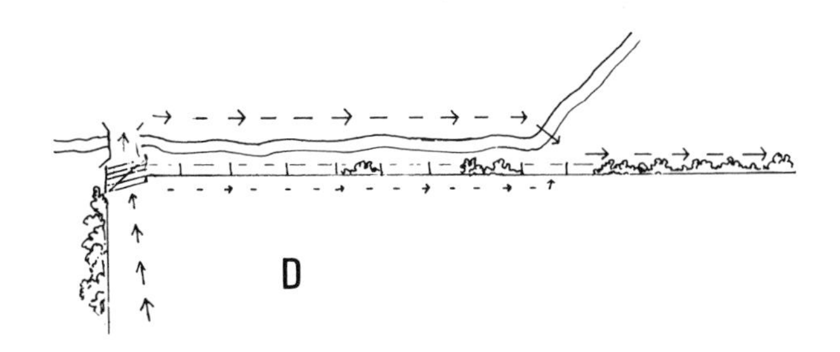

walk along it from the bridge to the bend, where you rejoin the legal right of way.)

Continue along a section with a hedge on your right and a field on your left. Then, at the point where you have a tree and a hedge ahead of you, pass to the right, so that you continue in the next field with the hedge on your left (*see* sketch E). Keep close to this hedge, which makes a number of turns, and at the corner of the field pass through the intersecting hedge and continue in the same direction as before, again with a hedge on your left.

After about 350 yards you will reach the corner of this field. The path continues between some bushes, and gradually uphill through a wooded area, following the same general direction, until it emerges on to a road.

Turn left along the road then almost immediately right, along another bridleway, through a wooded area. In a few yards you bear right, and continue with hedges on either side. Continue until you see a thatched cottage on your right, where the path turns left. If you stand with your back to the cottage you will see two gateways. The footpath goes through the right-hand gate. Go through this gate, taking care to close it as there are usually ponies in this field and cross the field. The path runs roughly parallel to the hedge on your left. Pass through the next gate and continue on the same line.

The next fence has a gate to the right of the actual line of the path; you may either climb the fence or detour to use the gate, to continue in

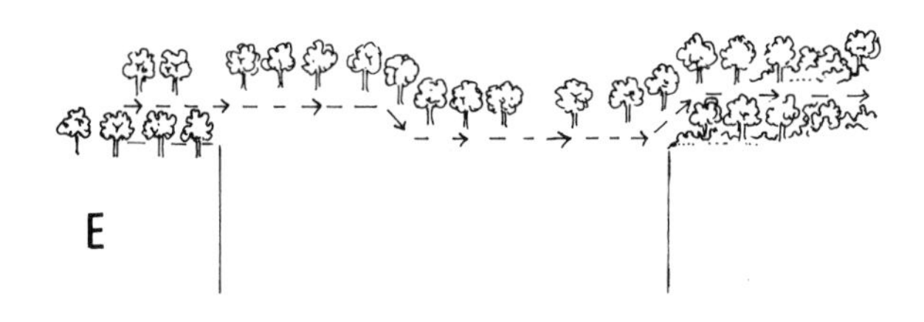

the same direction. At the corner of the next field there is a broken stile which you must negotiate before continuing in the next field with the woods on your left. When you reach the corner, note the 'Keep Out' sign on your left. Pass through the gap in the hedge in front of you, turn left, then, in a few yards, right again, keeping close to the woods and following the line of the ditch to your left. At the next intersecting hedge you pass through a narrow gap using a broken stile and continue in the same direction, passing a pond to your left, to a small gate. You then follow a short section of grassy track which emerges on to an unmade road close to Gregory's Farm.

Turn left along this road, which is fenced on both sides, and follow it when it turns right, keeping a hedge to your left. At the junction of tracks where there is a power pole, fork left, and continue down the road following the route of some power lines. There are open fields on each side and on your right is a view across to Watton and Bramfield Wood. Further along the road pass a trigonometrical point on your left and farm buildings on your right. Eventually the farm road swings right and emerges on to a lane. Turn right down this lane which is joined in a few yards by another lane from the left. Continue straight on downhill until you reach a major road. This is the Watton bypass. Cross over taking great care of the fast traffic, go through the gate opposite, and continue down the disused lane in the same direction as before and you will shortly arrive at your starting point in Watton-at-Stone.

Watton Church — Buckler 1832

WALK NO. 9

Green End to Haultwick

Green End – Haultwick – Green End

Distance 5½ miles

There is usually room to park at the side of the fairly wide lane that runs from the church up to Green End (GR 333221).

This walk starts about half a mile from Little Munden Church on the road that leads from Dane End to Green End.

Follow the road round its left-hand turn and then keep straight on.

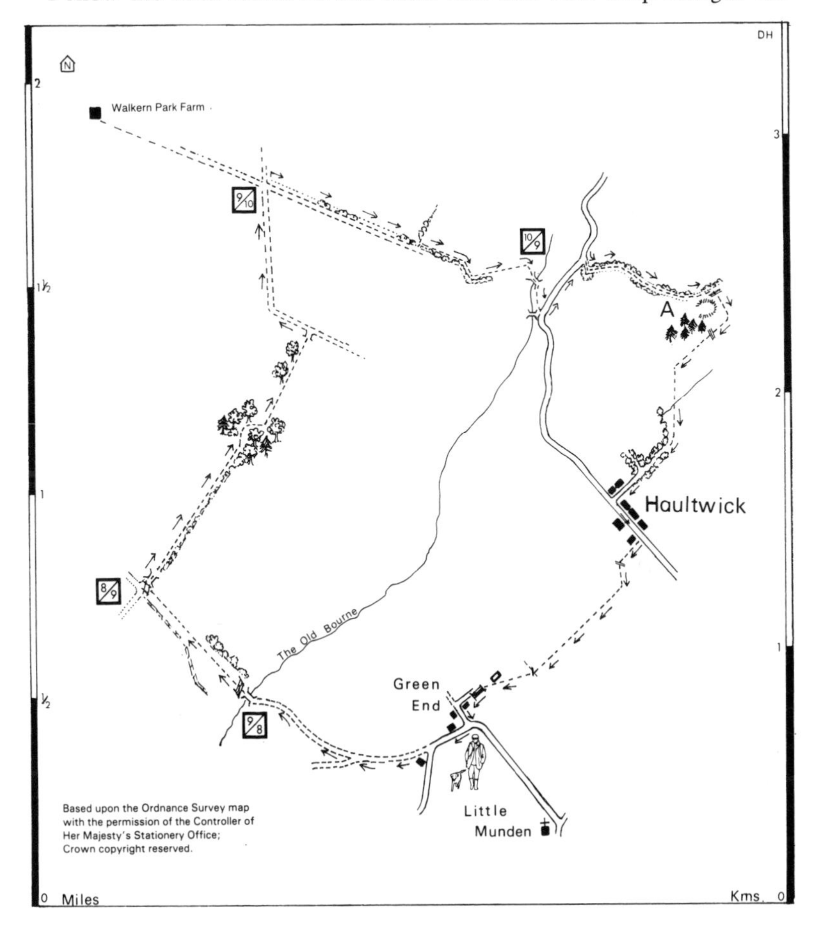

After about 50 yards you pass a pond on your right; wild irises grow here. At the point where the lane takes a left turn, where there is a house on the corner, go straight on along the track in front of you. Where the overhead cables cross the track you will see another lesser track forking right; take the right fork. This track goes gradually downhill and at the lowest point there is a river bed, usually dried-up. Cross the concrete bridge, 9/8 go through an iron gate and then immediately right, so that you now continue in a long wide meadow, in roughly the same direction as you were travelling previously. Usually there are cattle in this meadow and it is important to latch the gates at both ends. Part way along you will find that the meadow narrows and you are walking closer to the hedge on your left. This part is prone to flooding after very heavy rain. When you reach the far end of the field you will see a small gate in the left hand corner. 8/9 Go through the gate and turn right over a concrete bridge.

After crossing the bridge go straight up the hill in front of you, so that you have bushes and woods on your right and the field on your left. When you reach the top of the hill there are good views to your left. You reach a corner of the field where there are woods in front of you. Follow the path through the woods as it zig-zags and goes through brambles. Its course is often not obvious, in spite of the efforts of Footpath Society volunteers. Turn right when you emerge from the wood and follow it for a few yards to a point where the woodland bends. Here you bear a little to the left and walk towards a line of trees ahead of you. These mark the position of a hedge. Keep straight on with the hedge on your left and the field on your right. Where the hedge on the left ceases, cross an earth bridge over a ditch, on to a track, where you turn left. At the point where there is a barbed wire fence ahead, turn right with the track, so that you continue with a ditch on your left and the open field on your right.

At the next junction there is a track to the left, which leads to Walkern Park Farm, but you turn right. 9/10 The definitive map takes you downhill, keeping the ditch and the remains of a hedge on your right and the field on your left, but there is a track on the other side of the ditch; you can choose which looks the best option. If you are following the definitive route, after passing the overhead cables, go through the intersecting hedge and continue in the same direction downhill, with the hedge on your right and the field on your left.

Turn right where the hedge turns right and then, in a few yards turn left, so that you continue in the same field with the hedge on your right-hand side. You are going downhill to the valley of the Old Bourne. 10/9 When you reach the bottom of the hill, turn right and then, a little further on, cross the Old Bourne on a grassy track. (N.B. Some O.S. maps have omitted this path.) Keep on this track until you reach the road, where you turn left.

The road goes up a fairly steep hill. Go past one path marked on the

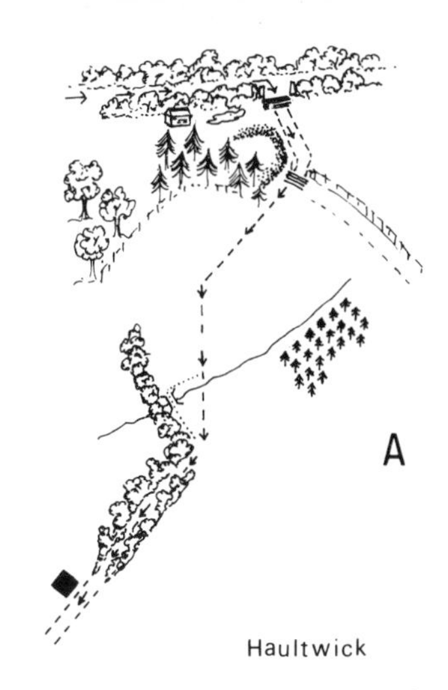

right-hand side before you reach the top of the hill. Take the next track to the right, which is at the top of the hill. This doubles back in the direction that you are travelling. A few yards along this path turn left, to follow a path which has bushes on either side. This path is a long steady uphill climb.

You reach a part where there are tall trees, a pond and then some farm buildings on your right. Nearby is a second pond and a wooden gate with a cattle grid on your right. Turn right through the gate. The field on your left is usually a green meadow and on your right there is a moat (*see* sketch A). Continue along the track, which bears right when you reach another gate with a stile alongside it.

There is a small plantation of trees on your right, and where these end you enter an open field, where it is often difficult to see the line of the path across the field. You will find that you are about 400 yards from some woods ahead and to your right. To the left there is a small plantation of fir trees and beyond that a ditch. The line of the path continues into the field in the same direction that you have been travelling along the track. The point to aim for is approximately half-way between the extreme end of the wood to the right and the nearest houses in the village. Continue in this direction until you are level with the end of the plantation of young trees on your left. Here you turn 45 degrees left, aiming for a sharp bend in the hedgerow in front of you.

Cross a deep ditch, which at present has no bridge*, and continue to the bend in the hedge, and then turn to follow the hedgerow as it turns right. Continue so that you walk along with the hedge on your right and the field on your left. Shortly the hedge on your right thickens, and it is in fact the border of a green lane with a double hedge. Choose the first opportunity to get into the green lane and continue in the same direction.

* A bridge has now been provided slightly to the west of the line of the right of way.

When you come to a junction of green lanes bear left. Continue on this green lane until you emerge on to a road in the village of Haultwick.

At the T-junction turn left, towards the centre of Haultwick, keeping a lookout on the right-hand side in about 250 yards for the footpath signpost pointing to 'Green End ¾ mile'. Turn right there so that you walk along a rather scruffy path, currently partly blocked by heaped earth, with a hedge on your right. You cross a small ditch and climb over a fence (which may be electrified) into the next field, continuing in the same direction, so that you have the field on your left and the hedge on your right.

At the corner of the field go over the fence where there is a broken stile and in the next field turn approximately 70 degrees to your left. You will see a big tree and, just to the right of it, a gate; make straight for that gate across the corner of the field. Climb over the gate (it is difficult to open) and turn right, so that you walk along with the hedge on your right and the field on your left. At the corner of the field there is another iron gate and broken stile. Bear very slightly to your right, so you continue in the next field again with the hedge on your right and the field on your left. Go straight on into the next field, where there is a broken stile at the end of a barbed wire fence. Continue with the hedge on your right and the field on your left. At the corner of this field there is sometimes a temporary piece of iron fencing, which you have to climb over, and you go straight on for a few more yards, when you will see another broken stile where you veer slightly to the right. You pass a pond or very marshy area on your right and you aim straight for the sports pavilion which you can see in the distance.

Walking across that field you pass the pavilion on your right and you come to a line of small trees, which you pass. Then turn right over a stile and left along a muddy track. This leads to a gravel lane between houses in Green End. When you reach the T-junction of lanes turn left. Very soon you come to another T-junction of lanes where you turn left again and you should recognise this as the lane on which you started the walk. In a few yards the lane takes a sharp bend to the right and you will be back at the start.

WALK NO. 10

Moor Green

Moor Green – Back Lane – Wood End – Sander's Green – Parker's Green – Muncher's Green – Moor Green

Distance 5 miles

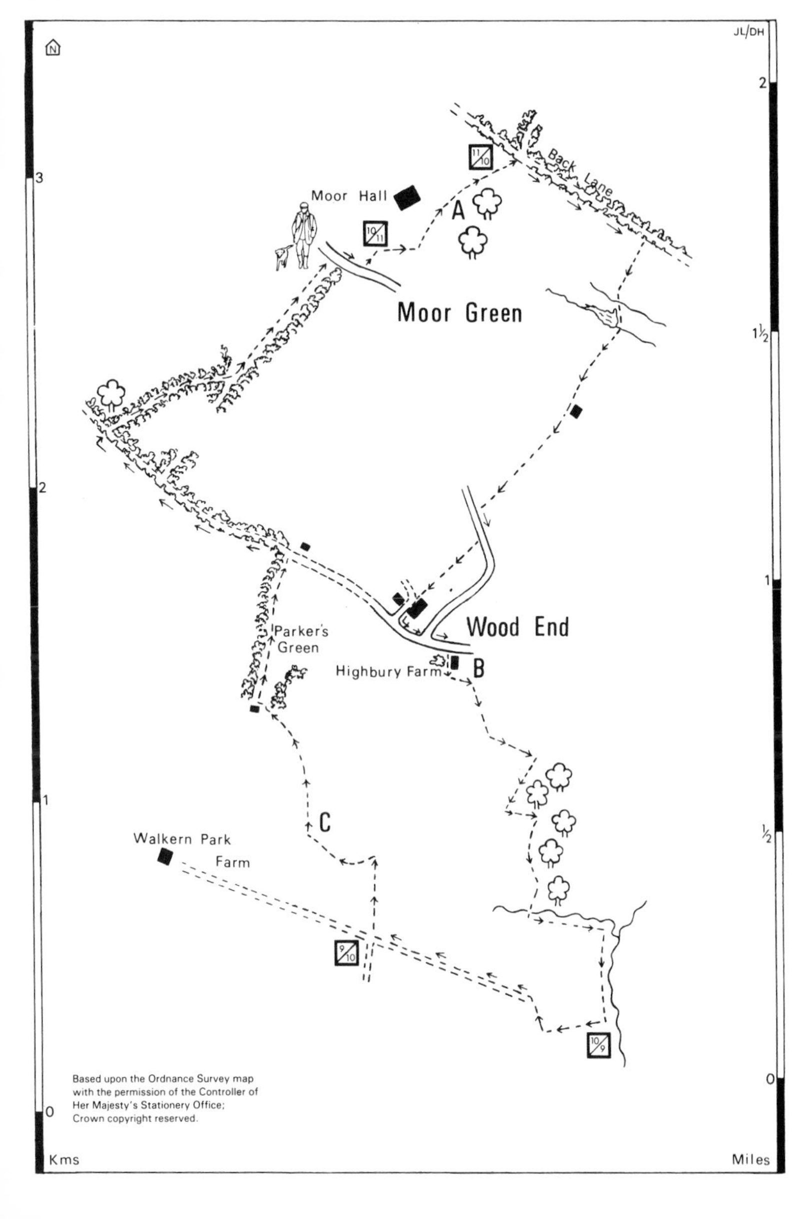

There is space to park off the road where it runs through the Green at GR 323267.

Moor Green is a hamlet halfway between Wood End and Ardeley, which, sadly, no longer possesses its own pub. Coming from Wood End the first house in Moor Green is The Goose, which used to be a public house until about 1980. Start from the middle of the Green walking south-east back along the road towards Wood End. Before you get to The Goose look for the gravel track on the left, where there is a 'Public Footpath' sign pointing towards a gate in the distance, beyond which are the low farm buildings of Moor Hall. Turn left along this track towards Moor Hall. As you go along the track you will see a white house and a small white bungalow across the green to your right. **10/11**

Go through the gateway and turn right, continuing with the hedge on your right (*see* sketch A). The path here is not usually visible. You pass close to a power pole on your right and go under electricity wires. Look for a wooden stile in the hedge on your right. Cross this stile and then turn left. As the hedge on your left curves away keep straight on, so that you gradually leave the hedgerow and cross the field diagonally, keeping to the left of a large tree in the middle of the field.

You gradually move away from the power line that you can see on your left and you get nearer to the woods on your right. You converge with a hedge on your left and in this you will see the wide gap of an old gateway. Go through it and then bear slightly right. Keep on a straight line which takes you to the corner of the woods and continue walking around the edge of the woodland for about 20 yards. Slightly to your left, about 150 yards away, you will see a gate. Veer away to the left to cross the field, passing under electricity wires, towards the small gate and stile. Cross the stile and turn right along the Roman road 'Back Lane'. **11/10**

Walk along Back Lane for about 500 yards, keeping a lookout, through the hedge on your right, for a point where there is a hedgerow going at right angles across a large field. At this point in Back Lane you should see a wooden post, on the left of the path, with blue and yellow arrows. Turn right and go through the gap in the hedge. With the hedge on your left and the field on your right you immediately pass close to a power pole with wires going in three directions. Near the next corner of the field turn left, and about 15 yards later turn right, across a broken stile in a barbed wire fence.

Veer left, then cross a muddy area, where there is a low wall and water to your right. Go on uphill through a small wooded area, keeping fairly close to the boundary on your right.

Aim towards a brick building, at present in a state of collapse, and close to it there is a barbed wire fence. Cross the stile in the fence into dense undergrowth just to the right of the building and make your way past the building on your left and continue with a hedge a few yards to

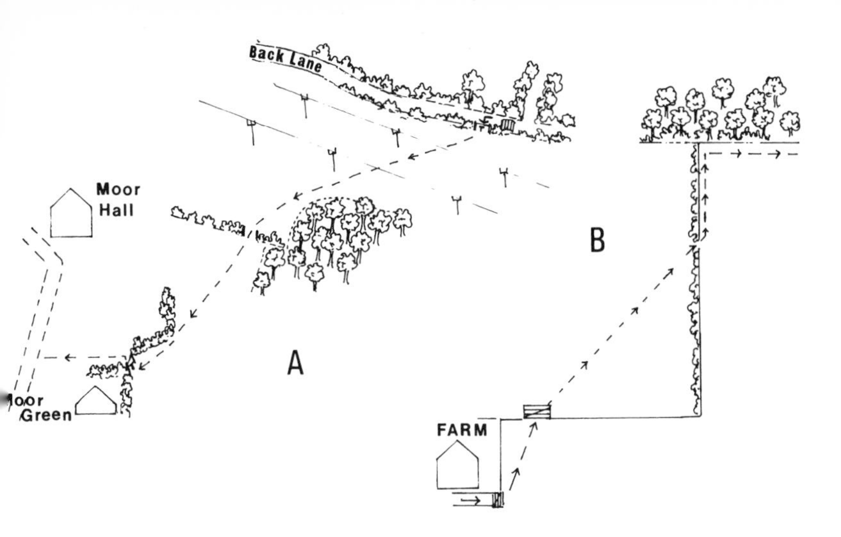

your right. You reach a deep ditch which has brambles and nettles on the near side and a hedge on the far side. Cross the ditch and pass through a gap in the far side hedge. You now have to maintain the same general direction across the large field you have entered.

Look across the skyline and notice a building slightly to the left and, to the right of that, some large trees. Further to the right you see a power pole and, to the right of that, two medium sized trees. Aim for a point just to the right of the right-hand tree. Just over halfway across the field look ahead of you for a metal barrier, and a footpath sign at the end of the field where the path joins the road.

Turn left at the road. About 75 yards further on turn right, just before the 'Wood End' sign. There are two field entrances. Go through the one on the left, where there should be a footpath signpost and cross the field diagonally. There are two power poles in the field and you aim for the furthermost one, which is at the end of a hedgerow. Pass close to that power pole and then follow the line of the overhead wires, passing a double power pole on your left. Keep straight on through the hedgerow and then along a short stretch between buildings on either side. This section is quite overgrown.

Turn left at the lane. At the junction of lanes keep straight on. About 200 yards past the junction and just after the overgrown duck pond, turn right at the signpost 'Footpath – Haultwick 1 mile'. Pass through the farmyard and an iron gate, then turn left, with a hedge on your left and head for a wooden gate in the corner of the field (*see* sketch B). Pass through the gate and then go 45 degrees right (you may have to cross a barbed wire fence), crossing the field diagonally. Aim for a gap in the hedge ahead of you, about halfway along the hedge. Go through the gap (there may be barbed wire here) and turn left, with the hedge on your left and the field on your right. Turn right at the corner of the field and proceed with woods on your left. At the next corner turn left, and at the

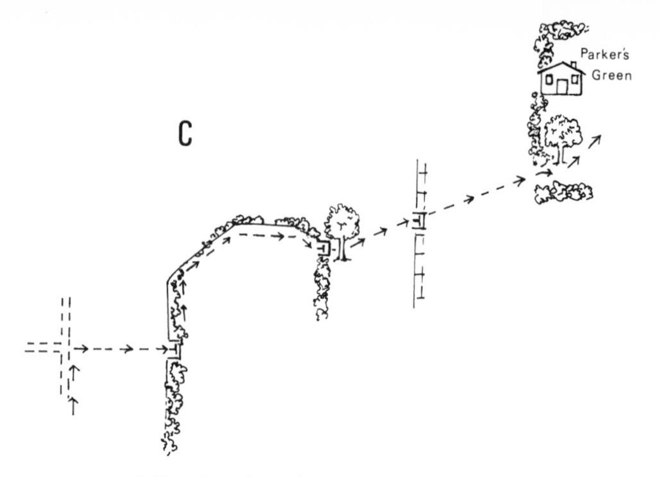

next one, following the edge of the wood, turn right. Go through an iron gate (frequently open) and turn left, with the hedge and trees on your left and the field on your right.

Turn right at the next corner and right again at the corner after that, walking uphill with the hedge on your left and the field on your right. **10/9** Turn right at the corner at the top of the hill, and about 60 yards later turn left, following the line of the hedge on your left. Good views here. At the next corner, where there is a double power pole, walk straight on through the hedge, keeping the hedge on your left. When the hedge peters out maintain the same direction going uphill.

At the top of the hill you reach a point where another bridleway joins from your left. **9/10** Turn right 90 degrees at this point, to make a continuous straight line with the bridleway that connected on your left. The path is not normally made-up here. Head towards the hedgerow across the field and find a gap in the hedge, which will be a few yards to your right (*see* sketch C). Go through the gap across a ditch, turn left and continue with the hedge on your left. Turn right at the first corner, right again at the next corner, and at the third corner turn left, across the remains of a stile alongside an ash tree on your left. Head for the stile on the far side of the field close to an oak tree. Cross that stile and maintain the same general direction across the next field, aiming slightly to the right of the pole which is itself a little to the right of a cottage surrounded by trees. Find a grassy track through the bushes just to the left of an oak tree. Follow that track to the green. Bear right so that you are now walking along the green path. Keep straight on at a junction of paths until the path becomes partly gravel. Continue walking along the track.

There is a complication with regard to the next section because the line of the public bridleway, according to the definitive map, runs about 4 yards to the left of the gravel track. The gravel track is private. The bridleway is now overgrown because travellers use the gravel track. The gravel track leads to a gate with barbed wire and a notice which reads

'Private Road to Greenlands'. The route of the bridleway bypasses the gate about 4 yards to its left, and re-joins the track at an open green (sometimes a bit overgrown), where you will see a red brick bungalow which frequently has a caravan parked beside it.

Make your way to the bungalow and turn left on to a track in front of it, so that the bungalow is on your right. Just before the track passes through a metal gateway into a field, turn left on to a bridleway which has a ditch on the right and bushes and trees on the left.

You need to walk along this bridleway for about a third of a mile to a point where it bends to the right and then to the left. Continue along this bridleway for another 170 yards and turn sharp right on to another bridleway. As you walk along, to your left in the distance, you should see the church spire at Ardeley. Continue, with small intermittent lengths of hedge on either side, for about 450 yards, and you then emerge on to Muncher's Green, just after an overgrown bridleway has joined you on your right. Keep straight on along the bridleway across Muncher's Green, veering slightly to the right of a hedge and trees in front of you. At the far side of the green the track that you are following makes a sharp right bend through a wide gateway. Do not pass through this gate but keep straight on along a grassy track, passing ponds on your left. This track can often be quite wet. You can see white houses in the distance as the track emerges on to Moor Green where you started the walk.

WALK NO. 11

Cottered going South

Cottered – Brook End – Flanders Green – Moor Hall – Cottered Warren Farm – Cottered

Distance 4¼ miles

It is best to park in the cul-de-sac lane that leads to Brook End (GR 323294). (This is the same starting point as Walk No. 12, Cottered going North.)

Cottered recreation ground is alongside the A507 road in the village of Cottered. 11/12 Walk eastwards, parallel to the main road, towards the phone box and turn right along the lane to Brook End, where there is a thatched cottage ahead. Turn right along a grassy and stoney track. Go through an iron gateway, where there is a small building with a cylinder-shaped corrugated iron roof, and turn left for a few yards along a track, so that you have a hedge on your left and allotments on your right. Go on to the drive of a bungalow. On the drive turn right and then left through the garden of the bungalow. About 15 yards after you have passed the end of the bungalow turn right through a white gateway. Bear slightly left to go across an open field aiming for the furthermost corner (*see* sketch A).

On reaching the corner of the field, go over the stile and turn right along a green lane. This is muddy in places. The path narrows and becomes more overgrown and then curves fairly sharply to the left. It then becomes a bit wider and crosses a small stream and you will see a cottage on your right-hand side. The path then meets a lane. Continue along the lane until you pass under electricity cables, at which point the lane bends sharply right. Eighteen yards after this turn left to leave the lane to go along a grassy track going gradually uphill. Keep on going with the hedge on your left and the field on your right (*see* sketch B).

When the hedge ends, carefully maintain the same direction across the open field. When you reach the far side of the field, find a gap close

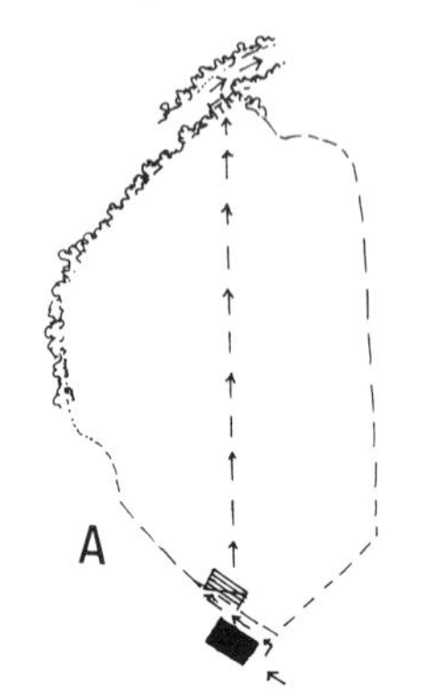

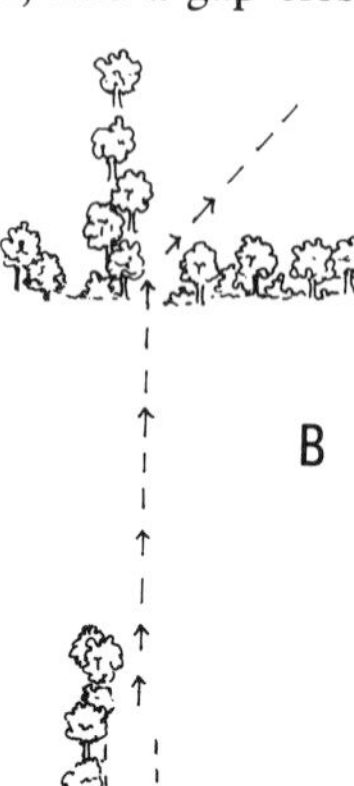

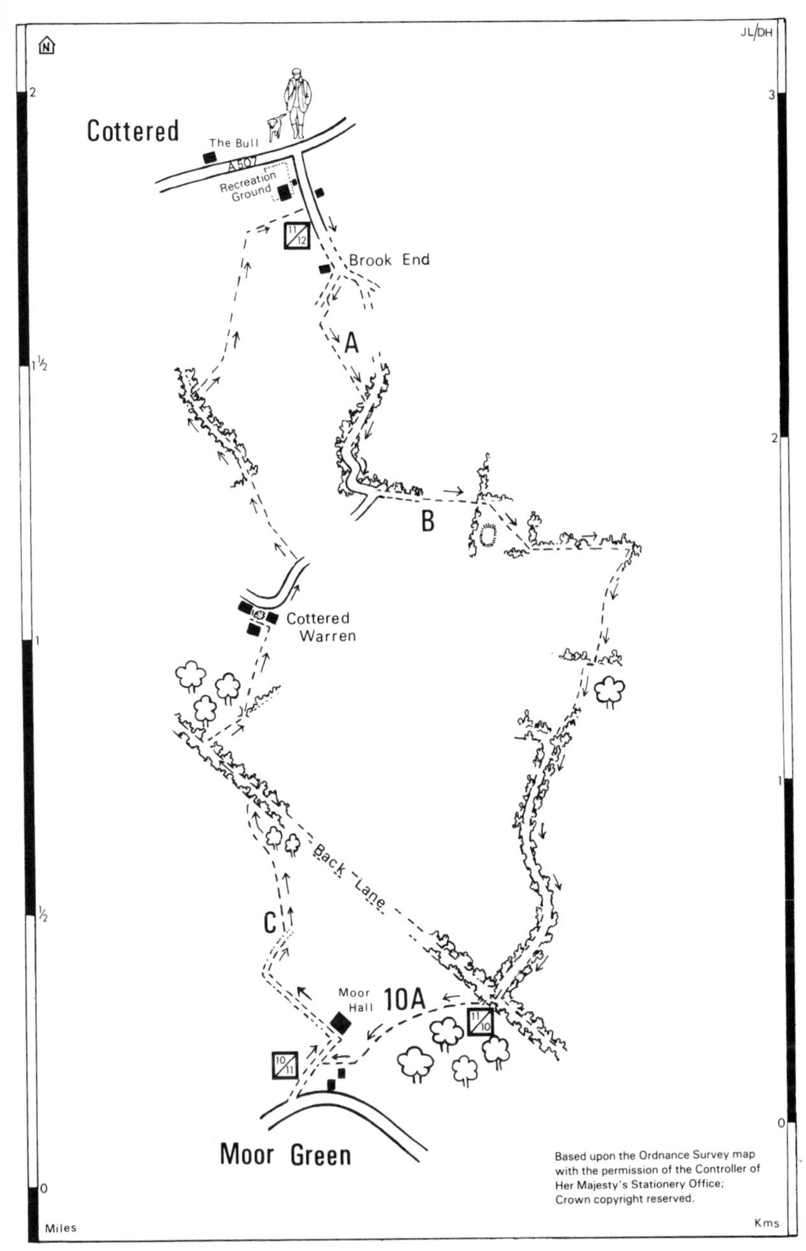

to the right-angled corner of the hedge. Go through that gap, which entails crossing a ditch within the hedge, and turn 45 degrees right, to cross the next field diagonally, and pass through an area recently planted with saplings. As you cross this field you gradually converge with the hedgerow on your left. When you meet up with the hedge at the corner of the field turn left down a steep bank to a ditch. Turn right along the ditch and in 8 to 10 yards find a single plank bridge. Cross the bridge and climb the bank to emerge into a field.

Turn left and proceed with the hedge on your left and the field on your right. At the corner of the field turn right, so that you continue with the hedge on your left and the field on your right. At the field boundary, find the gap in the hedge in front of you, go through, cross the ditch into the next field and continue in the same direction. You again have a hedge on your left and a field on your right.

At the corner of the field pass through the hedge by an old wooden gate post, and keep straight on, on to a raised path where you have a ditch on both sides. (This is a path which the East Herts Footpath Society used to clear by voluntary labour.) Keep straight on where the path has trees and bushes on either side. When you reach the T-junction of tracks turn right along the old Roman road 'Back Lane'. In a few yards cross a ditch on a wooden bridge and soon after that find a stile on your left. 11/10 Turn left to cross the stile and then turn 45 degrees right, to cross the field diagonally (*see* sketch 10A for previous walk). You go under power cables, pass a power pole on your right and aim for the corner of a wood. Gradually draw nearer to the wood on your left and bear left alongside the wood. A farmhouse comes into view. Gradually move away from the edge of the wood to aim straight for the farmhouse. Converge with the hedge on your left and go through the gap, which has an old wooden gate and gateposts. Continue diagonally across the next field, with the farmhouse about 100 yards to your right at your nearest approach to it.

This field has a number of dips in it. You gradually converge on the hedge on your right-hand side. Bear right fairly close to the hedge and in the corner of the field climb over a high stile near a new white bungalow. Turn left and continue fairly close to the hedge on your left and pass under electricity cables to reach a gateway on a track. 10/11 (If you wish to reach the road at Moor Green turn left along that track.) To continue to walk back to Cottered, turn very sharply right along the track, so that you are now walking directly towards the farmhouse. Just before you reach the farmhouse buildings turn left, so that you proceed with the black farm buildings on your right. Where the farm track bears right, at the end of the buildings, keep straight on along a grassy path, passing a clump of bushes which lies to your right.

You are now on a grassy track with no hedges. You pass a solitary tree on your right, near where the path makes a right-hand bend, and head towards a wood. Approximately halfway between the tree and the wood the path bears to the right again. At that point bear left, across the field, which may be ploughed or have a crop on it. Looking across the field you see power poles (*see* sketch C). You should be well to the left of the first pole in the middle of the field, and you must aim slightly to

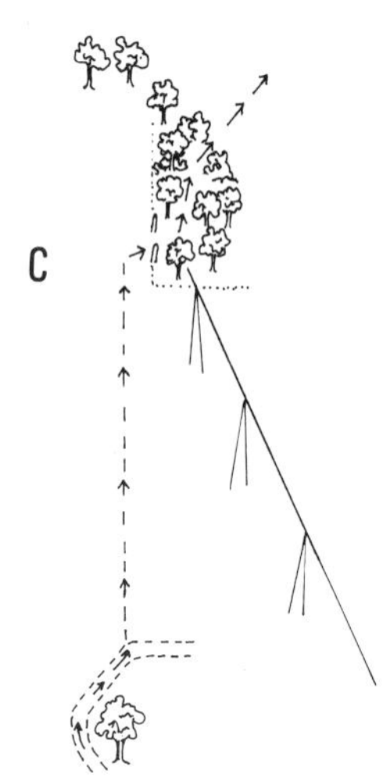

the left of the farthest pole, that is, towards the corner of woodland jutting into the field. When you reach the corner of woodland you will see the power pole 20 yards to your right. Bear very slightly left and continue for 10 yards with the woods to your right and the open field on your left. Turn right into the woods, passing an old wooden gate post on your right. In the wood, immediately turn left, through a generally overgrown area. Bear slightly right to cross the field, aiming for a stile which has some white paint on it. You gradually move closer to the electricity wires and you may find some pieces of fencing across the route. Cross a plank bridge and then the stile. Then bear very slightly right, aiming for a stile adjacent to a tree in the boundary hedge, and passing under the electricity wires on your way, cross that stile and turn left along Back Lane.

Back Lane is wet and muddy in places. Go approximately a quarter mile along Back Lane and turn right. The right turn is at a point where woodland starts on your right. After the right turn, you proceed with the wood on your left and a field on your right. Where the wood ends on your left, turn left over a wooden bridge across a ditch, and then immediately right into a field. Cross the field diagonally, aiming for the large grey building you can see in the distance. When you are close to the building turn left, so that you proceed with the building on your right. Walk through the farmyard. At the farmhouse turn right and when you reach the lane keep straight on, so that you pass the pond on your right. Do not take the lane going off to the left. In a little under 200 yards turn left at the signpost 'Cottered ½ mile'. You are now on a grassy track. Keep straight on where a ditch crosses and proceed uphill with the hedge on your left and the field on your right. You pass under electricity cables, pass a power pole in the hedge on your left and soon after that look out for a gap in the hedge on your left which gives access to the green lane. In effect you turn left through the gap, cross a ditch and then turn right to continue in the same direction, this time along a green lane. (This is cleared from time to time by volunteers from the East Herts Footpath Society.)

About a quarter mile along the lane look for a stile on the right in the barbed wire fence. Turn right to cross the stile and aim across the field for the nearest power pole. Pass close to the pole and maintain the same direction. You pass under another set of cables aiming for a tree in the hedge ahead. Turn left, to cross a small concrete bridge and a stile, and continue in the same general direction towards another stile you can see in the fence on the right-hand side of the field. Cross that stile and keep on going the same way. Cross another stile in the next hedge, turn right immediately and soon cross another stile into Cottered recreation ground from where the walk commenced. **11/12**

Cottered Church Doors — Aylott 1907

WALK NO. 12

Cottered going North

Cottered – Broadfield Hall – Whitehall Farm – Coles Green – Cottered

Distance 5½ miles

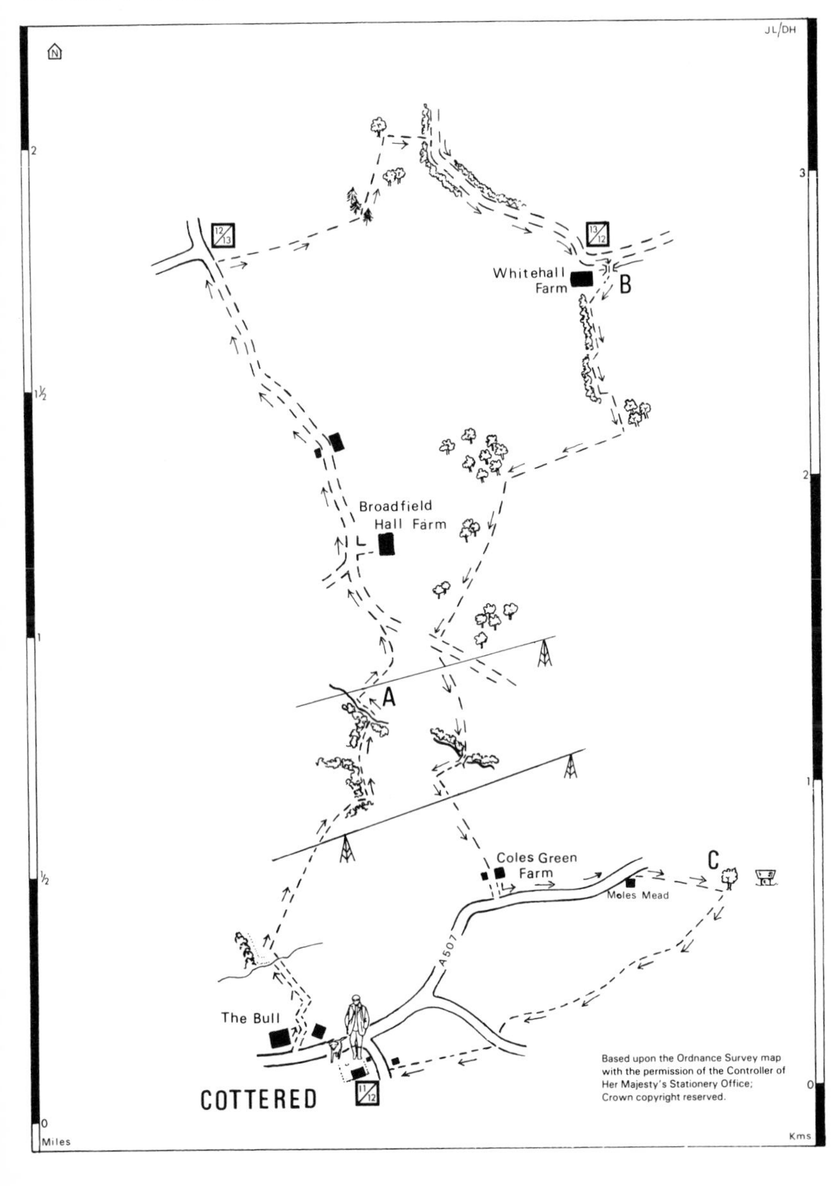

It is best to park in the cul-de-sac lane that leads to Brook End (GR 323294). (This is the same starting point as Walk No. 11, Cottered going South.)

This is another walk from Cottered Recreation Ground which is on the southern side of the A507 towards the eastern end of the village. 11/12

Cross the A507 and turn left. At the Bull public house turn right along a track beside the pub so that you pass the pub on your left with Glebe House on your right. You pass a signpost 'Bridleway to Broadfield Hall' and 10 yards on there is a turning to the right but you must keep straight on. (It can be muddy here in wet weather.) In about 20 yards bear right to stay on the track and in 40 yards stay on the track as it turns left. You have a hedge on the right and the track goes gradually downhill until you cross a stream (sometimes dried up) and emerge into a large field.

The field is crossed by two parallel sets of high-tension cables. Turn about 60 degrees right, so that you cross the field diagonally, going gradually uphill, aiming to the left of the pylon which is in the right of the field. You gradually converge with the high-tension cables to your left and pass under these where you have the pylon about 40 yards to your right. About 70 yards ahead you reach the corner of a hedge, and you continue with the hedge on your right and the field on your left. After 50 yards when you reach the corner of the field do not turn left or right but make your way through the bushes (there is a gap) in front of you.

Cross a ditch and when you emerge into the next field turn left. Continue with a hedge on your left and the field on your right. Where the hedge curves to the left leave the hedgerow, and keep straight on across a small piece of open field and on the other side turn right, so that you continue in the same field with the hedge on your left and the field on your right. When you reach the far corner of the field make your way through the bushes and trees ahead of you. Descend a steep bank to cross a ditch and climb up the other side. When you emerge into the field on the far side turn left. Continue with a ditch and hedge on your left and the field on your right. You will see a tall pylon in this field. When you reach the point where the hedge on your left ends and only the ditch continues, that is before you reach the overhead wires, turn 90 degrees right across the field (*see* sketch A).

Aiming for a wooden power pole, you pass diagonally under the cables and pass the pylon about 100 yards to your right. Soon after that you reach a metalled lane, and there you turn left. You keep on this lane in the same direction for a little more than three quarters of a mile, passing Broadfield Hall on your right and, much further on, reaching a section where the path has a concrete surface and there are old buildings on either side.

After that concrete section keep straight on uphill, where you have a bungalow and then a brick house to your right. As you are going up the

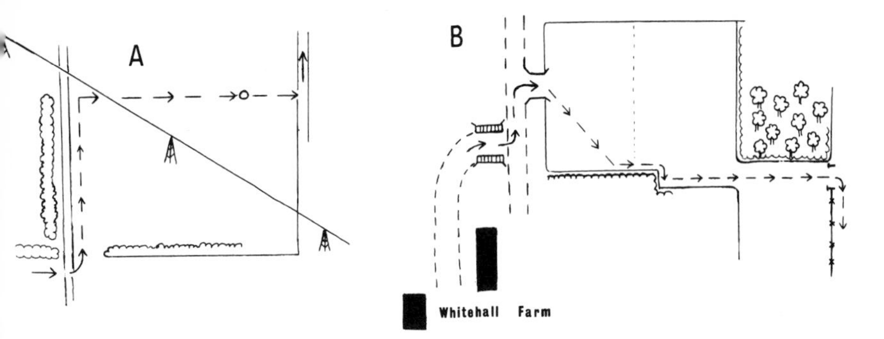

lane you will see ahead of you a junction of lanes with a signpost pointing to Rushden. Twenty yards before you reach the junction of lanes you will find an indentation in the bank on the right-hand side. 12/13

Turn 90 degrees right there, off the road, and you have to cross two large fields. Crossing the first field, you see ahead a line of trees, and you aim for the right-hand end of that line of trees, where you will find an earth bridge over a ditch. Cross the ditch and continue uphill across the next field in exactly the same direction.

At the top of the hill you will see a line of trees and a line of low bushes. Aim for the point where the line of taller trees, on the left, changes to lower conifers in a plantation, to the right of these. At that point, where there are two wooden posts, cross the ditch, and make your way through the bushes in front of you to enter a small plantation of fir trees. This feature may change in due course.

Turn diagonally left, approximately 45 degrees, picking out the best route between the trees, and in a few yards you reach a field. You need to maintain the same direction and so you cross the field diagonally (*see* sketch C for Walk 13). Looking across the field you can see the point where the line of trees and bushes to your left comes to an end. Aim for that point, and as you cross the field you pass within 25 yards of a pond, surrounded by bushes, to your right. When you reach the point aimed for, you will find a ditch with an earth bridge. Do not cross the bridge but turn diagonally right, so that you continue with a ditch on your left and the field on your right. When you reach the corner of the field, find a way through the clump of bushes in front of you, cross a steep ditch approximately five feet deep, and then turn right along a track. The track goes downhill, and in 70 yards you turn left, to continue on a grassy track with a ditch on your left and the field on your right. 13/12 At the corner of the field, where you see farm machinery, turn right. In 50 yards turn left on to the concrete surface between farm buildings. You pass a newish bungalow on your left and grey buildings to your right (*see* sketch B). The path curves round to the main track with a low brick wall on both sides. Turn left on to a concrete track, and in 50 yards turn right, on an earth bridge over a ditch.

Turn diagonally right, aiming for the hedgerow. A fence once halved this field and this path follows the old route to the corner of the first field. At the edge of the field, turn left, so that the hedge and ditch are to your right. Continue along the edge of the field, where the hedge turns right, then left, to resume the same direction. At the corner of the field pass through the gap, to continue with the woods on your left and the field on your right. At the next corner of the field, turn right and cross the barbed wire fence, so that you continue with a barbed wire fence on your right and a field on your left.

Where the fence makes a right-angled turn, continue straight on across an open piece of field, aiming for a point where the wood ahead becomes a row of trees and bushes. When you reach the far side of the field, go through the gap in the hedge and emerge into the next field.

There you will have the wood on your right. Turn approximately 60 degrees left to cross the field diagonally. In the fields beyond there are high-tension cables, and you will be aiming for a point where the cables are at their lowest, midway between pylons. As you proceed you pass a large clump of trees just a few feet to your right. Still maintaining a straight line, continue down a dip, passing roughly midway between a small woodland on your left and another clump of trees on your right.

Keeping parallel with the wood on your left, as you go uphill you will be 100 yards from the wood and fifty yards from some trees on your left, and approaching high-tension cables ahead. You do not cross them in this field. You may need to find your way through a tall crop at the end of this field to reach the lane.

At the lane you will see an old white gate to your right, and fields ahead. Beyond the field you can see another set of cables and two distant pylons ahead. In the field on the other side of the lane turn 45 degrees left. Aim one third in from the left pylon and two thirds from the right pylon, as you cross the field diagonally. You pass under cables as you proceed. You gradually converge with the hedgerow to your right, and, when you reach it, turn right to cross the footbridge, which is hidden in the hedge.

At the next field go straight ahead for 125 yards, aiming slightly to the right of a distant pylon. As you proceed you may see a church steeple ahead in the distance. When you are halfway to the pylon turn left. The ground rises ahead and as you get to the top pass under the power cables. Ahead you will see a gate leading to a farm. Pass through the gate and then between the farm buildings and soon after emerge on to the road.

To shorten the walk, you can turn right here, to walk down the road to where it meets the main road. This is the A507. Turn right (towards Cromer), and walk the remaining half mile along the road to return to the start of the walk.

To continue on the original route, which is about a half mile longer, turn left along the road to a point where the road bears left and on the right is a house, Moles Mead. Fork right there through the wooden gate

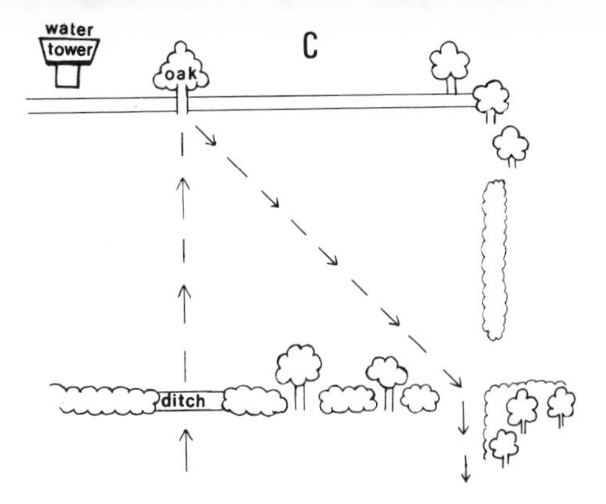

(not the gate to the house), and cross the field diagonally, aiming for the furthermost corner, where there is a clump of trees.

Pass the trees on the right and cross a ditch into the next field. Continue in the same direction across this field, aiming for the large oak tree ahead (*see* sketch C). There you will find a ditch and you are in line with a water tower further to your left.

Here you virtually about-turn to your right, and cross the same field again, but aiming for the field corner opposite. This is the corner that was 90 degrees to your right when you first entered this field.

At the corner of the field bear right, continuing to follow the line of the hedge on your left. When the hedge ends, keep straight on with open fields on both sides. Before the hedge recommences, cross to the left side, to follow with the hedge on the right and an open field on the left. At the corner of the field, continue in the same direction (ditch and hedge on right), into the next field.

Where the hedge and ditch curve to the right, leave the line of the hedge and cross the field, aiming to the left of the houses and straight towards a power pole. Cross the road and continue with hedge and houses on the right. At the corner of the field, bear right then left, down a garage drive. At the road turn right. You will then see the telephone box just off the A507 at Cottered. Turn left to return to the recreation ground. **11/12**

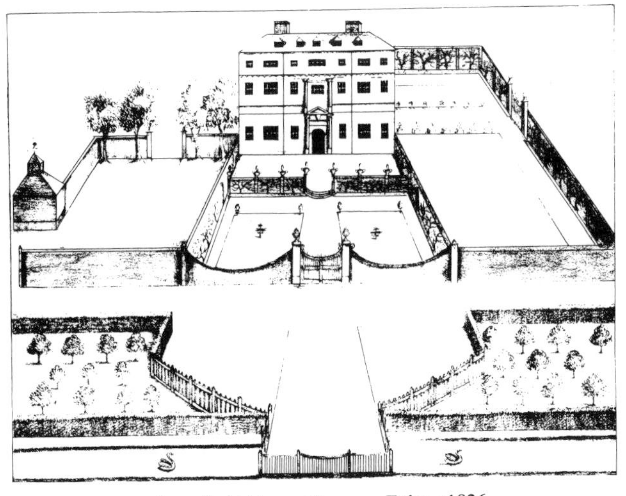

Broadfield Manor House — Tyler *c.*1826

WALK NO. 13

Sandon going South

Sandon – Beckfield Farm – Mill End – Whitehall Farm – Roe Green – Sandon

Distance 4¾ miles

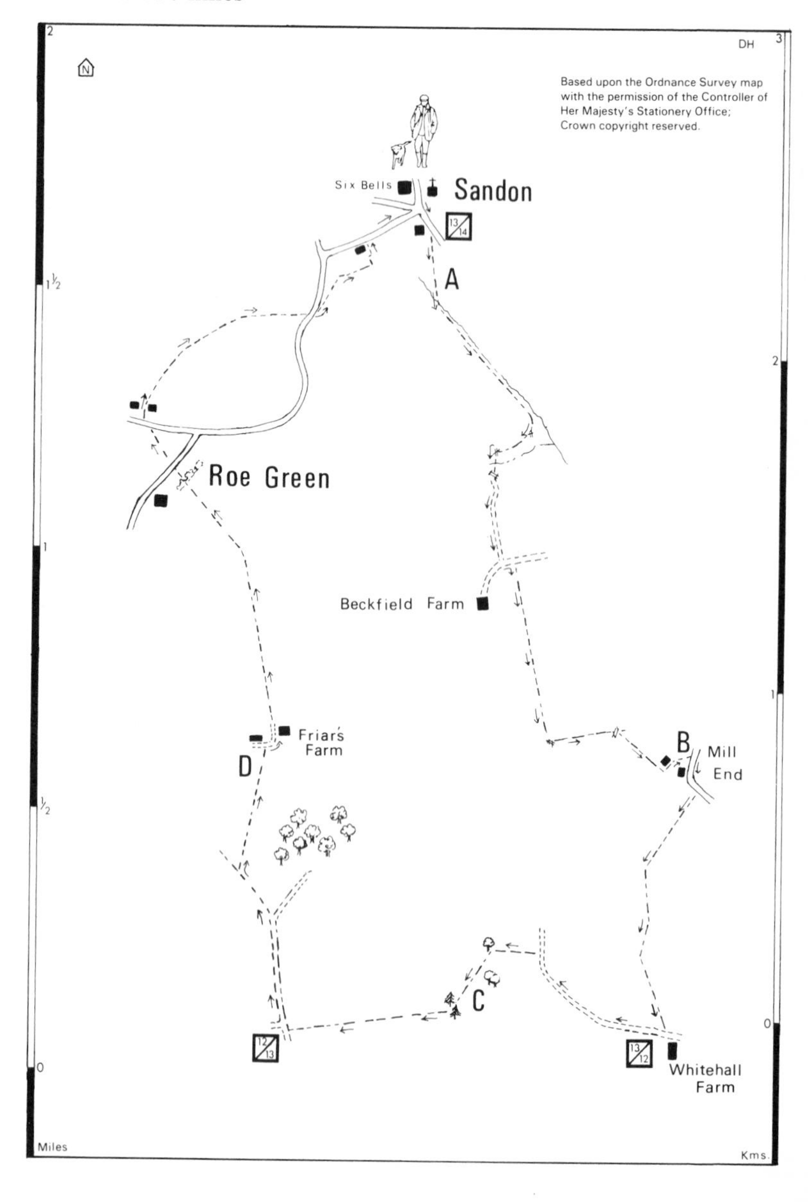

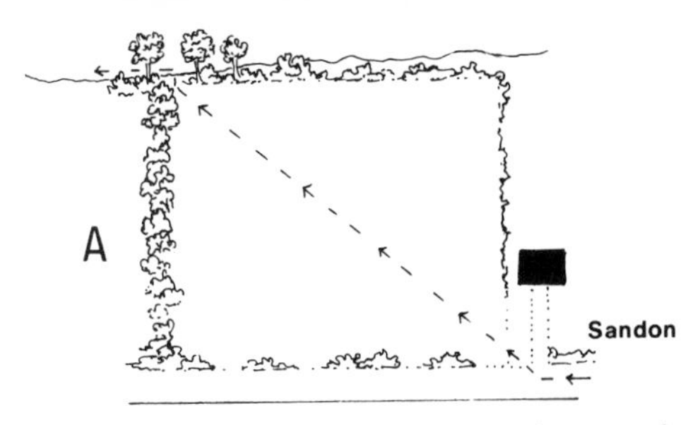

There is usually room to park near the church or alternatively on the triangle of lanes that serve the village (GR 320344).

The walk starts on the road between the church and the Six Bells public house.

Walk south towards the signpost and take the lane towards Buckland and Buntingford. 13/14 In a few yards, at a point where there are farm buildings on your left, you will see a house to your right. Take the rough track which leads towards the left-hand side of this house (*see* sketch A). When you enter the field bear slightly left and cross the field diagonally, aiming downhill to the furthermost corner, where there are some birch trees. This path is sometimes ploughed or has a crop on it. At the corner of the field cross the ditch in front of you and turn left. You continue with the hedge and ditch on your left and the open field on your right. Keep to the edge of the field, as it makes several bends following the line of the ditch.

When you reach the corner of the field turn right, going uphill, with hedge on your left and the field on your right. Pass a stile on your left and continue uphill. Pass under electricity wires and a few yards after that you will find a second broken stile on your left, at a point where the hedge makes a 90 degree turn to the right. (You may have to penetrate stinging nettles to reach it.) Turn left to cross the stile which takes you into the adjacent field, keeping the hedge on your right and the field on your left. In a few yards you will cross a ditch, and, a few yards further on, find a gate in the hedge on your right.

Turn through the gate, remembering to close it behind you, and then immediately turn left. In this field you go uphill slightly, with the hedge on your left. The path soon takes a right bend, then a left bend, and you continue to have the hedge on your left. You will be walking towards some farm buildings. You eventually emerge on to a narrow lane and turn left. In about 60 yards, at the next telegraph pole, turn right, into a large field with a paddock on your right. Continue with a wooden fence on your right and the field on your left. Where the fence on your right ceases, keep straight on across the open field. As you progress aim for the right-hand end of the line of trees in the distance. When you reach a fence on your left-hand side, continue in approximately the same direction, following the line of the fence on your left.

You will be going downhill to the corner of the field and there turn left, through or over a gate. (At the time of writing this gate was padlocked and had barbed wire on it.) Keep going with the hedge on your right and the field on your left. In a few yards you pass a gateway on your right but ignore this and keep going straight on to the next gate on your right. Go through this second gate. (Please do not forget to close it behind you.) Once in the field, bear diagonally left up the hill, heading for the houses just visible on the top of the hill, and aim for the roof of the right-hand building (*see* sketch B).

When you reach the brow of the hill you will be able to see a fenced garden with a house beyond. (The path on the definitive map runs through the garden to the roadway but is, at the time of writing, obstructed.) Continue with this fence on your left. Pass the end of a low building and then turn left through a gate just beyond it. Walk along beside the building and at the far end turn right over two sections of fencing, into a narrow way with a hedge on your left and fence on your right. In a few yards you will find the entrance to a short narrow path, with hedges on both sides frequently overgrown with brambles. You emerge on to a lane and turn right.

Go uphill along the lane for about 100 yards and then turn right at the footpath just before the next group of buildings. This is usually a well-defined track going uphill. At the brow of this minor hill to your left you will see a ridge with three or four trees and, at present, an electrified fence. Turn left there, going downhill, with the ridge on your left and the field on your right. At the corner of this field you cross a ditch and an electrified fence into the next field. Look down the hill towards some farm buildings. The line of the path is difficult to follow across this field as the path is usually ploughed or has a crop on it. Aim for the right-hand end of the farm house you see in front of you.

When you reach the far side of the field, cross a ditch and stile, and turn right along a grassy track. (There may be some wooden barriers you will have to cross.) 13/12 You will be going gradually uphill, away from the farm, following the line of the ditch on your right-hand side. The track makes a number of curves, and eventually takes a right turn, which you also take, going a little more steeply uphill. There will now be a ditch and hedge on your left. About 75 yards after the right turn, look carefully across the ditch on your left, to where the fields on your left are divided by a ditch and hedge. At this point turn left, crossing the ditch which you have been following and then passing through a clump of bushes, to emerge into a field where you should have a ditch on your right and the field on your left (*see* sketch C).

The ditch on your right eventually enters a small tunnel and you come to a clump of bushes and trees. At the time of writing there is a lone oak there. Turn approximately 45 degrees left, crossing an open field, which is often ploughed or has a crop on it. You pass close to a small pond surrounded by a clump of bushes about 20 yards to your left as you cross the field. You should be aiming towards a small plantation of

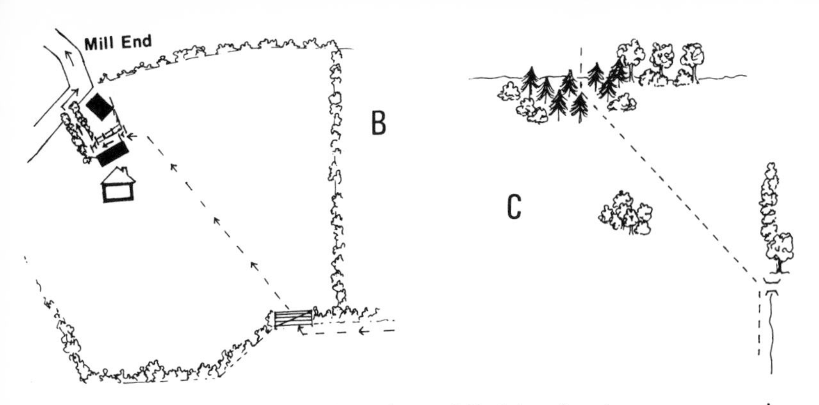

fir trees. (These trees may have been felled by the time you are using this book.) When you reach the plantation make your way through the trees, maintaining the same direction until you can see the opening on your right into the adjacent field.

Bear right there, cross the ditch, and in the next field, which is very large, and where the path is often ploughed or has a crop on it, you aim straight across the field, leaving the hedgerow directly behind you. As you cross the field, at the point where it slopes downwards you will see that there is a hedgerow, which has some tall trees. Aim for the left end of the tall trees. When you reach that point, you will see that there is an earth bridge over a ditch, which you cross. Keep on in exactly the same direction. On the far side of the field you emerge on to a lane and turn right. 12/13 A few yards on, at the junction of lanes signposted 'Wood Farm Only', keep straight on. When you reach the junction of tracks where the concrete path turns to the right, keep straight on, along a grassy track, thus leaving the lane with the made-up surface. About 60 yards along the grassy track you emerge into a field, where you bear left, along the boundary of a field, so that you have a ditch and hedge to your left.

As you proceed keep a watch on the ditch to your left, until you reach a point where there is a junction of ditches and hedgerows. (At this point another footpath crosses but it is often ploughed or has a crop on it.) Turn right, away from the ditch and hedge, to cross the open field. On the skyline you will see a long bungalow and you aim just to the right of this (*see* sketch D). Close to the bungalow you emerge on to a gravel track, which bears right a few yards along, to bring you close to the

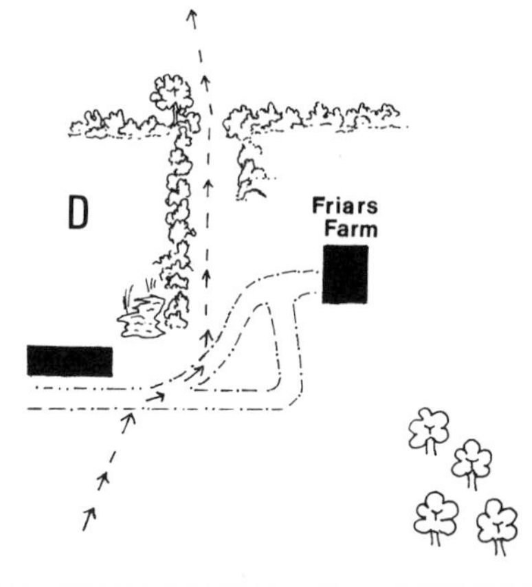

outbuildings of a house on your right. Turn left, to pass between the long bungalow and the outbuildings of the house. Keep left, leaving the path, and proceed along a grassy area with a hedge on your left.

At the point where the hedge ceases there is an ash tree and you emerge into a large field. The path is across this field, which is often ploughed or has a crop on it. Maintaining the same general direction, go out into the field. You can aim at a point to the left of the large tree in the distance. The field is crossed by two ditches, both of which you have to cross. The first ditch runs only part-way across the field and you should cross this ditch about 50 yards from its right-hand end. You will now be able to see overhead power lines and you must look for the pole with double insulators where the cables slightly change direction. Aim for that pole. A little to the right of that pole is a bridge across the second ditch, by a small tree. Cross the ditch and bear very slightly left and look in the distance for a gap in the far hedge. You may be able to pick out the white goal-posts in the recreation ground beyond the hedge, and beyond those the gable-end of a light-coloured house. Continue across the field, aiming for these landmarks.

Pass through the gap in the hedge and emerge on to Roe Green and maintain the same direction. Cross a lane, and soon after that pass in front of the sports pavilion. Proceed diagonally across the green, the old tennis courts being to your left. Emerge on the road close to the tennis courts. Across the road is a dwelling known as Tay House, which has an area of bushes and a small hidden pond to its left. You need to find the footpath at the back of Tay House. You reach it by keeping close to the line of bushes to the left of Tay House and crossing a piece of rough ground passing under electricity wires.

Then turn right, and a little way along on the left, between hedges, you will find a stile. Turn left to cross the stile, and continue into the field with a shallow pond on your left and a line of small trees and fence on your right. There is a new fence directly ahead of you with a stile mid-way along it, cross this and continue into the next field. Where the fence on your right ceases, bear very slightly right, aiming towards a large oak, just beyond which you will see a gate with a stile alongside. Cross the stile and again bear very slightly right. Sandon church is now clearly in view. You will gradually converge with the fence and hedge on your right. Look for the stile in the wooden fencing. You cross this and a ditch and a second section of wooden fencing, to reach the adjacent field. Bearing very slightly left as you go uphill, you again gradually converge with the fence and hedge, this time on your left, until you reach the gate at the corner. Emerge on to the road and turn left.

Almost immediately turn right, and, after crossing the broken stile, turn left. You proceed with a hedge on your right and just a little way from a hedge on your left. When the hedge on your right ceases keep straight on across the small field, resisting the temptation to turn left towards the Chequers public house! On the far side of the field find a piece of wooden fencing with, three feet beyond, a piece of iron railing with a broken iron gate. Crossing the wooden fencing and going through the iron railing into the playing field of the school, skirt round the field, keeping the iron railing on your right and the school on your left. Eventually, when you reach the kissing gate on the far side of the playing field, turn through this gate, and immediately turn left, and continue with the railings on your left. Cross a small stile and pass between some wooden sheds and the iron railings. You pass close to a house on your right which is the village store and Post Office. Emerge on to the road which, if you turn right, leads you back to the start of the walk.

Monumental Brasses, Sandon Church

WALK NO. 14

Therfield going South

Therfield – Kelshall – Sandon – Therfield

Distance 5 miles

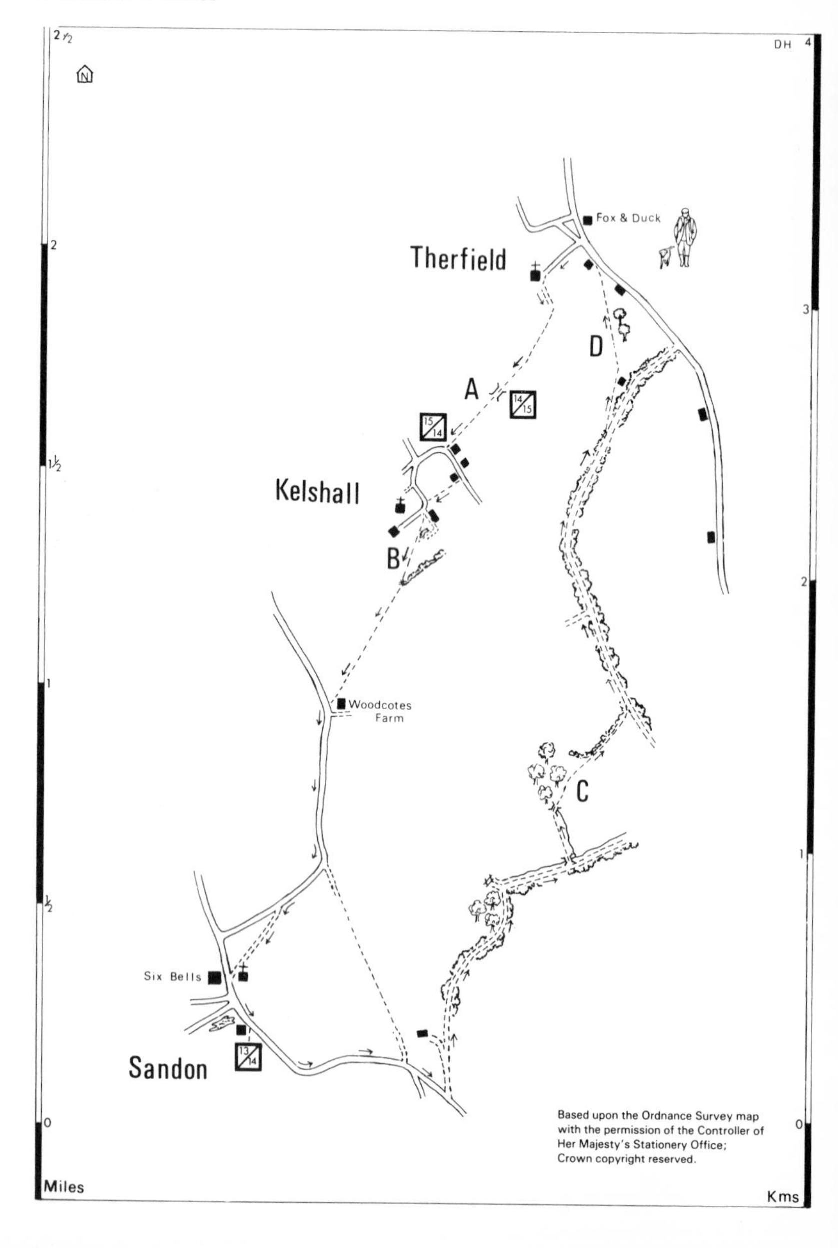

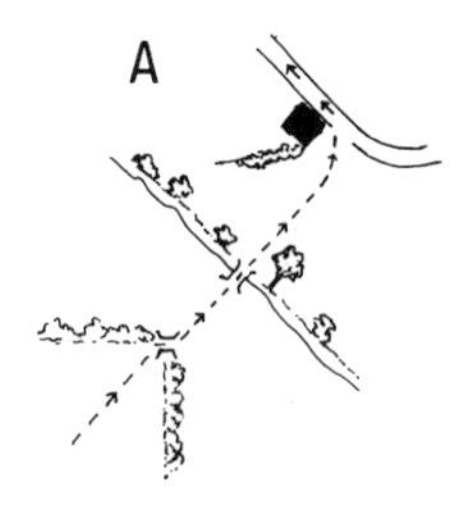

There is usually room to park near the village green which is situated opposite the Fox and Duck public house (GR 336372).

This walk starts from the Fox and Duck public house, Therfield. Walk directly away from the Fox and Duck across the road. Pass the wooden Therfield sign and continue down the road indicated by the sign 'Church – No through road' and known as Church Lane.

Walk towards the church and pass the footpath signpost 'Northend Kelshall' and enter the churchyard. Pass the church on your right. As you are passing the church turn left, so that you go through a gap in some iron railings and go away from the church. You are now on a grassy track, with railings and a house on your left and a field and hedgerow on your right. When the track reaches the next field turn 45 degrees right, to cross the field diagonally, aiming for the furthermost corner, where you see a power pole. At that corner you will find a small earth bridge over a ditch, and an old broken gateway, which takes you into the next field.

You now face a large open field which you must cross in approximately the same direction as you have been travelling. On the distant horizon you see houses, and where a clump of trees rises higher than the houses you may be able to see the top of Kelshall Church tower. Aim straight for that. To get across the ditch running through the field, look for a small solitary tree with two power poles to the right of it (*see* sketch A). Your route should take you a little to the left of that tree. When you reach this point you will find there is a wide earth bridge over the ditch. 14/15 Maintain the same direction and pass under two sets of electricity wires and gradually approach a house which has gable ends. Near the house you emerge on to a lane 15/14 and there turn left, to pass in front of the house. Pass another house on the left called The Maltings (which has a civic award) and, just beyond a new bungalow on your right, turn right on to a public footpath.

You now have a hedge and bungalow on your right and field on your left. Where the hedge on your right ends continue in the same direction across the open field, aiming just to the right of some trees on the right of a row of timber-clad houses. On the far side of the field you will find a footpath signpost and a gap in the hedge, which allows you to emerge on to a lane. There turn left. Almost immediately turn right as the lane bends to the right. You pass one of the timber-clad houses and outbuild-

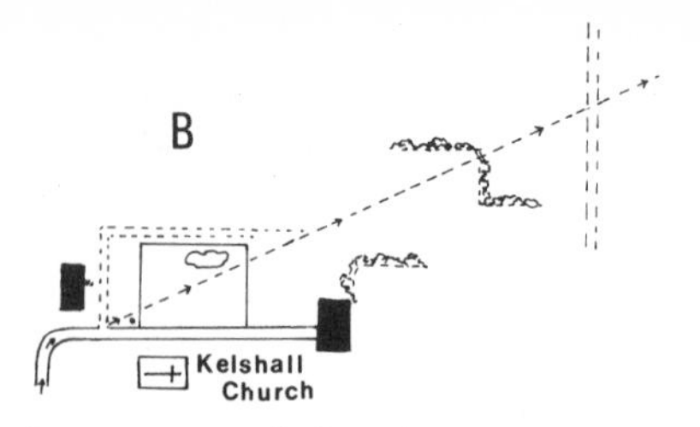

ings on your left and as soon as you have passed them fork left, so that you go just to the left of a telegraph pole (*see* sketch B).

At this point the land crossed by the footpath has been fenced off to make a garden but stiles have not yet been provided. Cross the timber fence and enter an area of well-trimmed grass and continue in the same direction, moving gradually away from the lane and the church, which are to your right. You pass a pond on your left just before you reach a second timber fence. Cross that and proceed in the same direction, to cross a small field diagonally, aiming for the distant corner. As you proceed you pass within 50 yards of the corner of a hedge on your right. You gradually converge on a hedge to your left and aim towards a clump of trees, just where there is at present an old broken stile without a step. Cross the stile and continue in the same direction. You see ahead a large field which rises uphill and on the skyline some farm buildings. Aim just to the right of those buildings.

Part-way across the field you cross a farm track. Good views here. Continue to aim to the right of the farm buildings, towards the corner made by two hedgerows which should now be clearly visible. At that corner there is a wet muddy area. Pass by a tree close to a ditch and you emerge on to a road alongside a signpost. Turn left along the road and pass in front of the farmhouse. Pass a house called Fallowfields on your left. Stay on the lane where it curves to the right. When you reach the 'Sandon' sign fork left, to go gradually uphill along a narrow path with hedges on both sides. You emerge into the churchyard and continue in the same direction, passing the church on your left. Pass through the church gate and emerge on to the road opposite the Six Bells public house, and turn left. 13/14 At the road junction keep straight on, the road being signposted 'Buckland and Buntingford'.

In just over half a mile fork left at a road junction, turning left after about 100 yards along a track where you will have a green on your left and bushes and woods to your right. At the next junction of tracks fork right, on a rougher path uphill through woods. This is a very wet and muddy path. Keep on the path between bushes and do not enter the field on your right. Eventually you have woodland on your left and further on the path does a right turn. Turn right there to stay on the path, do not go through the gate ahead. Continue with bushes on both sides.

Four hundred yards after the right bend, turn left through the bushes on your left, to reach a ditch where there is a broken bridge, which may be difficult to find. Cross the ditch, and continue with a field on your left and another ditch and sparse hedge on your right. You are walking towards a small woodland. When you reach the corner of the field at the woodland turn right, crossing an earth bridge over the ditch. You continue with woods on your left and the field on your right. Curve slightly to the left to follow the edge of the wood, but, at the point where the boundary of the wood makes a right-angled turn to the left, proceed across the open field, maintaining the same direction (*see* sketch C).

As you are heading towards a row of medium-sized trees on the far side of the field you will meet up with a hedgerow where it makes a right-angled bend. There, bear very slightly right to continue downhill with an open field on your right and the hedge on your left. At the corner of the field fork left along a muddy grassy track which is usually clearly visible. It passes over an area of rough ground and continues as a wide gravel track between hedges and ditches.

At the point where the main gravel track makes a turn to the left you go straight on, leaving the gravel track, and continuing on a grassy muddy path with a thick hedge on the left and a sparse hedge and bank on the right. This path is very muddy in patches and winds gradually uphill with trees and bushes on both sides. You reach a point where there appears to be a path crossing, and, looking across the field to your right you see farm buildings and houses while in the field on your left you see a power pole. Here you keep straight on uphill, with trees and bushes on both sides. You next come to an area which opens out to a wider area of grass, and across the open field on your right you see farm buildings. On your left is a gate.

Turn left to go through the gate and then immediately fork right to cross the field diagonally, and aim for the furthermost corner of the field (*see* sketch D). Pass through the hedge at the corner of the field where a new stile has been provided, and in the next field continue in approximately the same direction towards the gate. You pass under electricity cables and then pass through the gateway. In the next field turn slightly left. You aim towards a large tree beyond which, slightly to the right, is a house. As you proceed you gradually move further away from the electricity cables which you see to your left. The path follows a line of a slight indentation in the field and has a number of old trees along it. Keep straight on and you pass the house on your right-hand side, along the path where you have a hedge on your right and the field on your left. At the corner of the field you cross a piece of iron fence and continue past a double power pole over a grassy area to the road.

When you reach the road turn left, to return to the Fox and Duck.

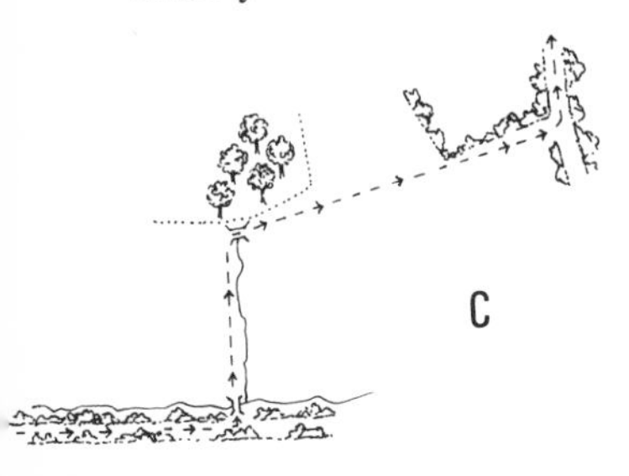

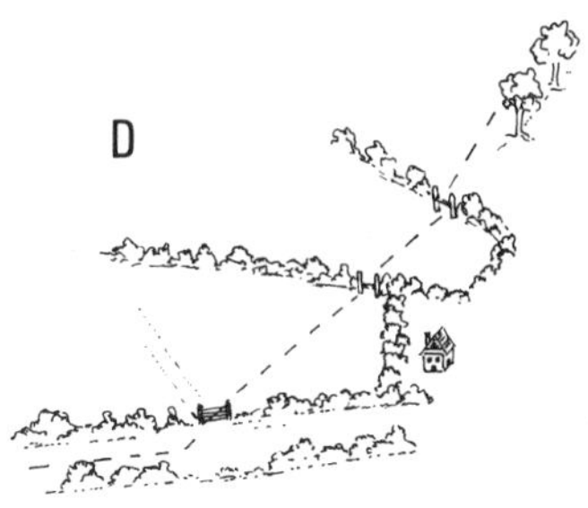

WALK NO. 15

Ashwell Station to Therfield

Ashwell (BR) Station – Gallows Hill – Stumps Cross – Kelshall – Therfield – Ashwell (BR) Station

Distance 6½ miles

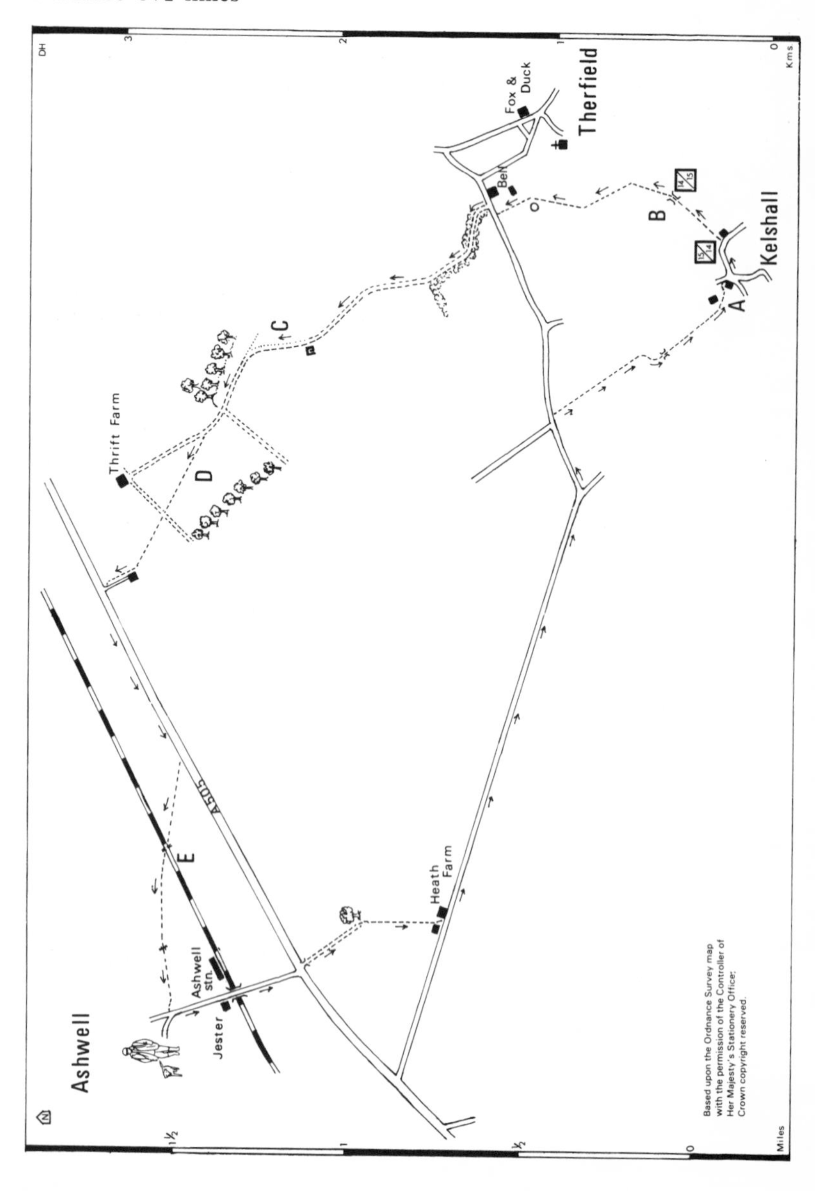

There is a car park at Ashwell (BR) Station and it is also possible to park in the road, preferably to the north of the station.

This walk starts from Ashwell BR Station. Anyone wishing to start from Therfield should commence from the Bell public house.

Walk south along the road from Ashwell Station, using the pathway which runs along the right-hand side of the road. After passing the Jester public house you reach an intersection with a dual-carriageway road (A505). Go straight on here, crossing the main road carefully, and enter the field opposite, using a path which crosses a ditch on an earth bridge. Go straight on, uphill towards a clump of trees; there are good views from the top. Pass the trees on your left and proceed downhill towards some farm buildings. Keep straight on across a lawn, between a bungalow on your right and the farm buildings to your left, then on to a road, where you turn left.

Regrettably, there is a fair amount of road on this walk and you now start the longest section of it. Continue steadily uphill on the road for 1¼ miles, taking an occasional look back at the view across Cambridgeshire. At the road junction turn left, where there is a signpost to Therfield. There is now a good long-distance view to your left. At the next junction, when a lane joins from your left, keep straight on for 55 to 60 yards, then turn on to a footpath on your right. You climb a low bank and then proceed along the edge of a field, with a dip and, a little later, a hedge on your left, and on your right, an open field.

Further on the path goes downhill. At the bottom of this hill, where there is a corner, turn right for a few yards and then left, to follow the line of the ditch and hedge on your left once more. In a few yards you cross a ditch by an earth bridge, where there is usually an abundance of stinging nettles. Continue in the same direction in the next field, still with the hedge on your left. The path goes gradually uphill. Where the hedge ends, about 70 yards after the earth bridge, keep straight on uphill across the open field. Veer very slightly left and pass close to a solitary tree and you should now be able to see a stile in the fence ahead of you. (At the time of writing this stile has no step.) Cross the stile and continue in the same direction across the next field, aiming for another stile with no step.

Just before you reach the second stile you will cross a gravel track and see some farm buildings on your left (*see* sketch A). Cross the stile and continue on for 10 yards, then turn left in a grassy area, where there is

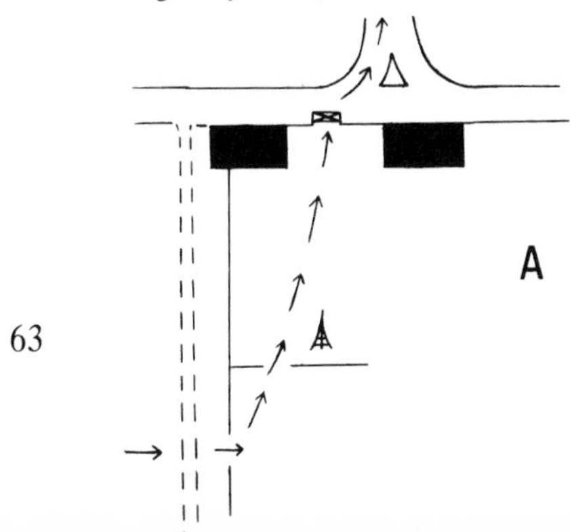

usually some farm machinery. In about 60 yards you reach yet another stile, similar to the previous two, which is in a hedge. Cross this stile and enter a small field where you should see a power pole about 20 yards to your right, a new bungalow ahead of you and some older buildings slightly to the right of that. Aim for a point between the bungalow and the older buildings. On the far side of the field you emerge, by a gateway, on to a road close to a road junction.

Go straight along the road ahead of you signposted 'Kelshall Street'. This takes you downhill past a 'No Through Road' traffic sign to your right. As you approach a large house the road curves to the right and just before you reach this house you turn left into a field by a signpost 'Public Footpath – Therfield'. **15/14** This path does not go along the edge of the field but follows a route bearing slightly left across the field and is not easy to find (*see* sketch B). Looking across the field, you can see Therfield Church and, to the right of the church, the roof of a large house beyond some trees. Aim for the point midway between the church and the house.

As you proceed you will pass under two sets of electricity cables. Ahead of you is a ditch, with the remains of a hedge alongside it. You should cross the ditch over an earth bridge, marked by a gap in the thin hedge. **14/15** From the bridge veer slightly more to the left, aiming for a point between the church and the water tower to its left. When you reach the hedge on the far side of the field turn left, so you continue along the edge of the field with the hedge on your right. At the corner of the field climb a small bank and through a patchy hedge into the next field, and immediately turn right, crossing a stile and a small plank bridge over a ditch. Then turn sharp left into yet another field.

You can now see the water tower clearly. Aiming just to the right of it, cross the field diagonally. Near the tower some allotments cause a small unofficial diversion: turn right, then left, on to a well-defined track and proceed along it, passing the water tower on your left. Further on there is a large thatched building on your right, which is well worth a look. Eventually you reach a road where you turn right; there are good views across Cambridgeshire from here.

At the bottom of a dip in the road you will find a narrow path between some bushes on your left, turn left down this path. Should you reach the Bell public house, you have come too far along the road and will have to retrace your steps for a few yards back to the footpath, which is just to the west of the pub.

Follow the path, which has an overgrown hedge on each side, until you reach a point where there is a gate ahead and a pond on your right. Turn left here. The path goes gradually downhill. There are still hedges on both sides, it is often overgrown with nettles and brambles and some parts may be muddy. Eventually you emerge at the corner of a field and here you must continue in the same direction, following the hedge on your left. Curve gently to the right, following the line of the

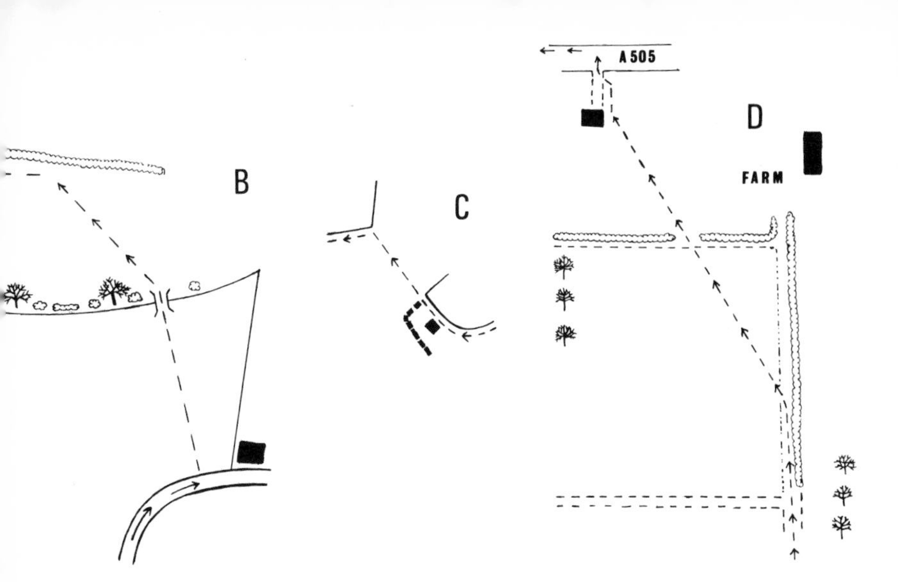

hedge, and continue this slightly curving route across the open field when the hedge ends. You will be aiming for the lowest point in a large bowl formed by the contours of this prairie-like field.

As you proceed, the land on either side of you gradually becomes higher than the path, which now begins to curve to the left, heading towards a small escarpment with bushes growing along it. As you near the escarpment the path curves a little more to the left. You now continue along a grassy track with the field on your left and the rising bank on your right. Further on, the track takes a bend to the right, to follow the line of the bank on your right. Just after this, there is an area with dilapidated buildings and a wall on your left. You then reach a section where the path is sometimes not visible on the ground, but maintain the same direction across the field to reach another small escarpment where you make a very slight left turn, and continue with a fence on your right (*see* sketch C).

Beyond the bank on your right make a note of a clump of trees further up the hill. On your left, at this point, there is usually a farm track, which leads to the end of a line of trees. From this spot go straight on for another 100 yards, then fork left off the track, to cross the open field diagonally (*see* sketch D). You will see a gap in the hedge ahead of you and beyond that a house; line up with the gap and the house so that you can keep a straight line as you cross the field. The line of the path goes down a dip, then rises, and you will see farm buildings over to your right. Cross a farm track and then climb the iron fencing in the gap in the hedge. Maintain the same direction in the next field, aiming for the right-hand side of the house. Near the house you cross a fence, and proceed so that you pass the house on your left. Just before the main road (A505) you cross a stile on your left and emerge on to the main road.

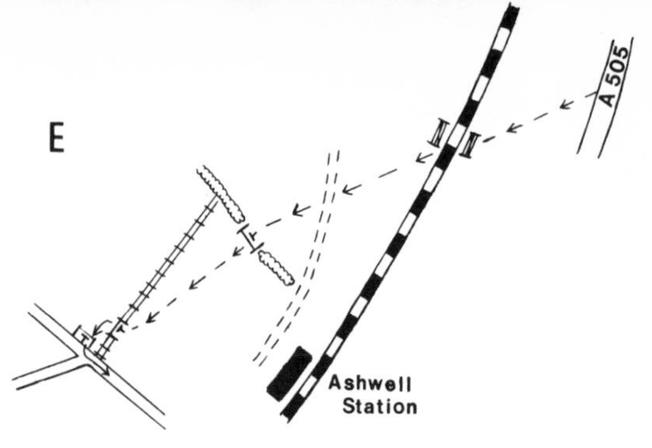

Cross the A505 and turn left, to continue along the grass verge with the carriageways on your left. Keep straight on where the road to Therfield joins on your left, until you pass the 'Therfield' traffic sign. (N.B. You approach on the blank side of the sign.) A few yards past that sign you should find a gap in the hedge on your right. Go through the gap, and cross the field diagonally, at an angle which is 40 degrees to the hedge now on your left (*see* sketch E).

You go gradually uphill and when the ground levels out you will see the overhead wires of the railway ahead. You may also note the remains of a tumulus on the higher ground to your right. Aim for the white post by the railway-line and here you cross over the railway, using the two gates provided. Take care and look both ways before crossing as trains can approach very swiftly from either direction.

Once safely across the line resume the direction you were taking in the previous field, aiming for a small gap in the hedge ahead. Before you reach this gap you pass under some electricity cables and cross over a gravel track. Go through the gap in the hedge and aim for the far corner of the next field, just to the right of a double power pole. Shortly before you reach the corner of the field, you will find a stile (with no step) in the barbed wire fence on your right. Cross the stile and turn left to a second broken stile which you negotiate to emerge on to a road. Turn left along this road to return to Ashwell Station and the Jester public house.

Kelshall Church Cross